SAVING LIVES AND

MICHAËL NEUMAN
FABRICE WEISSMAN
(*Editors*)

Saving Lives and Staying Alive

Humanitarian Security
in the Age of Risk Management

Médecins Sans Frontières

HURST & COMPANY, LONDON

First published in the United Kingdom in 2016 by
C. Hurst & Co. (Publishers) Ltd.,
41 Great Russell Street, London, WC1B 3PL
© Médecins Sans Frontières, 2016
All rights reserved.
Printed in the United Kingdom

Distributed in the United States, Canada and Latin America
by Oxford University Press, 198 Madison Avenue, New York, NY 10016,
United States of America.

The right of Médecins Sans Frontières to be identified as the authors
of this publication is asserted by them in accordance with the
Copyright, Designs and Patents Act, 1988.

A Cataloguing-in-Publication data record for this book
is available from the British Library.

978-1-84904-651-0 *paperback*

This book is printed using paper from registered sustainable
and managed sources.

www.hurstpublishers.com

ALSO FROM MSF-CRASH
(Centre de Réflexion sur l'Action et les Savoirs Humanitaires)

François Jean (ed.), *Populations in Danger*, London: John Libbey, 1992.

François Jean (ed.), *Life, Death and Aid: The Médecins Sans Frontières Report on World Crisis Intervention*, London: Routledge, 1993.

Fabrice Weissman (ed.), *In the Shadow of "Just Wars": Violence, Politics and Humanitarian Action*, London: Hurst & Co., 2004.

Xavier Crombé and Jean-Hervé Jézéquel (eds), *A Not-So Natural Disaster: Niger '05*, London: Hurst & Co., 2009.

Jean-Hervé Bradol and Claudine Vidal (eds), *Medical Innovations in Humanitarian Situations: The Work of Médecins Sans Frontières*, New York: MSF-USA, 2011.

Claire Magone, Michaël Neuman, Fabrice Weissman (eds), *Humanitarian Negotiations Revealed: The MSF Experience*, London: Hurst & Co., 2011.

This book is available online at www.msf-crash.org

CONTENTS

CONTENTS

PRACTICES

ABOUT THE AUTHORS

Monique J. Beerli is a PhD candidate in Political Science at the University of Geneva (Global Studies Institute, GSI) and at the Institut d'Études Politiques de Paris—Centre d'études et de recherches internationales (CERI).

Delphine Chedorge is a former emergency coordinator at Médecins Sans Frontières France.

Jonathan Edwards is Advocacy and Public Affairs Manager at Médecins Sans Frontières Australia.

Duncan McLean is a former Programme Manager at Médecins Sans Frontières France. He is a lecturer in history at the Anglo-American University, Prague.

Michaël Neuman is a Director of Studies at the Centre de Réflexion sur l'Action et les Savoirs Humanitaires, Fondation Médecins Sans Frontières.

Judith Soussan is a Director of Studies at the Centre de Réflexion sur l'Action et les Savoirs Humanitaires, Fondation Médecins Sans Frontières.

Bertrand Taithe is Executive Director of the Humanitarian and Conflict Research Institute (HCRI) at the University of Manchester.

Dr. Mego Terzian is President of Médecins Sans Frontières France.

Fabrice Weissman is Coordinator of the Centre de Réflexion sur l'Action et les Savoirs Humanitaires, Fondation Médecins Sans Frontières.

TABLES AND FIGURES

LIST OF MAPS

LIST OF ABBREVIATIONS

AWSD	Aid Worker Security Database
CAR	Central African Republic
CRG	Control Risks Group
ECHO	European Commission's Humanitarian Aid and Civil Protection Department
FIDH	Fédération internationale des Ligues des droits de l'Homme (International Federation for Human Rights)
GPR 8	Good Practice Review Number Eight
HO	Humanitarian Outcomes
IAO	International Aid Organisations
ICRC	International Committee of the Red Cross
ISIS	Islamic State of Iraq and al-Sham
MDM	Médecins du Monde
MSF	Médecins Sans Frontières
NATO	North Atlantic Treaty Organisation
NGO	Non-Governmental Organisation
ODI	Overseas Development Institute
SiND	Security in Numbers Database
UN	United Nations
UNDSS	United Nations Department of Safety and Security
UNICEF	United Nations Children's Fund
UNWFP/WFP	(United Nations) World Food Programme
USAID/OFDA	United States Agency for International Development/ Office of U.S. Foreign Disaster Assistance
WHO	World Health Organisation

ACKNOWLEDGEMENTS

This book is a collective effort.

Members of the CRASH Scientific Committee Marc Le Pape, Bertrand Taithe and Claudine Vidal and our colleagues Jean-Hervé Bradol, Rony Brauman and Judith Soussan from CRASH have all made invaluable contributions to this project.

In various ways, and in different capacities, many friends and colleagues have provided valuable assistance with re-reading the different chapters and contributing their questions and comments. We would like to thank academics Christine Fassert and Renée Zauberman who took the time to discuss our initial research and answer our questions. We owe particular thanks to Benoît Leduc who, as the first "security focal point" and then deputy executive director of MSF's French section, has supported our endeavour and largely contributed to its realisation. We are also grateful to Sarah Imani who generously designed the maps that accompany some of the chapters of the book.

Caroline Serraf organised the translations, which were proofread and edited with virtuosity by Ros Smith-Thomas. This book would not have been possible without the enthusiastic collaboration of Médecins Sans Frontières' coordinators in the field and at headquarters.

All are warmly thanked.

Michaël Neuman and Fabrice Weissman
Paris, October 2015

PREFACE

Mego Terzian

President of Médecins Sans Frontières, France[1]

When MSF nurse Chantal Kaghoma regained her freedom in August 2014 after being held hostage for thirteen months by rebel group ADF (Allied Defence Forces) in the Democratic Republic of Congo, she said, "While I was in prison with all the other hostages, I had lost all faith in everyone. Deep down, I no longer believed in MSF. I thought to myself, 'Well, it's all over now; this is the end.'" Then she added, "But, even though I no longer believed in MSF, I found myself coming to its defence." Three of our colleagues are still being held by the ADF and the organisation continues its efforts to track down their location and secure their release. A specially dedicated team has been working tirelessly for more than two years with the firm conviction that a positive outcome is possible.

This example reflects the principles that guide MSF in managing the security of its international and national staff. Chantal, like any MSF volunteer, is aware of the risks inherent to our deployment of relief operations in environments destabilised by war, epidemics or natural disasters. While there is no such thing as zero risk, she also knows that our practices are geared towards reducing danger. We gauge these dangers against the results we expect to achieve with the populations we serve and launch operations only when we are able to clearly identify the authorities with whom we can negotiate the safe access we require to deliver our medical assistance. We also endeavour to put together teams suited to the settings in which we work, in terms of numbers

PREFACE

and skills. Lastly, and maybe most importantly for Chantal's colleagues who
are still being held captive, MSF does everything in its power to secure as
quickly as possible the release of its staff.

We firmly believe that, for our relief operations to be effective and serve
their intended purpose, we must rely largely on teams of volunteers assisting
people in the field. Since the organisation was founded in 1971, violence has
claimed the lives of thirteen international personnel and many more national
staff members. Over the past few years, MSF's French section has experienced
numerous security incidents, including kidnappings, robberies and attacks on
our hospitals. We have developed a number of tools for managing security: an
incident database created by the Belgian section in 2009 was rolled out in
2013; specific security modules have been added to existing staff training
programmes; and we have updated our official policy on risk-taking in the
field, which reaffirms the principles shared by all members of the Association. Lastly, we have produced a handbook that provides guidelines on kidnap
resolution. All of these responsibilities are assigned to a "security focal point",
a position created for the first time in our section's history in 2013.

We are not, however, completely satisfied with these developments. We are
especially concerned about the exponential growth of procedures and documents designed to oversee the work of our colleagues in the field. Many of
these procedures and training courses convey the impression that the inappropriate behaviour of volunteers is primarily to blame for any violence committed against them. This perspective holds that they need to work under the
supervision of a higher authority, particularly that of managers at headquarters wanting to follow security-expert recommendations to the letter. I do not
share this view and I hope that the organisation is able to distance itself from
such a centralised and dehumanised approach to humanitarian action.

In saying this, I am well aware that we are not always able to do better than
others in meeting all the challenges involved in keeping our volunteers safe.
We cannot deploy international staff to Syria or work in Somalia and we were
probably overly cautious in our response to the Ebola epidemic. We have,
however, been effective in other dangerous situations: in Gaza during Israel's
"Protective Edge" military operation; in Central African Republic; and, more
recently, in the centre of war-torn Yemeni city Aden.

We must analyse unsparingly our past experiences and draw the necessary
conclusions to improve our practices. For that reason, I asked CRASH to contribute to the reflection on staff security and the place of risk management in our
projects. This book is the result and I share both its findings and its perspectives.

Its findings, because they show that the dominant risk-management culture is not up to the task of providing convincing answers to the concerns of aid workers. And its perspectives, because I am convinced that we can better ensure team and project security by placing our trust in those who run the projects in the field and that we, as a group, must show ourselves to be capable of discussing openly and collectively each of our very unique experiences.

1

HUMANITARIAN SECURITY
IN THE AGE OF RISK MANAGEMENT

Michaël Neuman and *Fabrice Weissman*[1]

In 2013 the French section of Médecins Sans Frontières (MSF) created the position of "security focal point," tasked with developing guidelines, procedures, a database and training courses for security management. In so doing, the section joined the rest of the MSF movement, which, like other large humanitarian organisations and corporations, had already set up safety and security units or departments dedicated to risk prevention and management.

Encouraged by Western donors, the field of security expertise for NGOs and UN agencies took off in the mid-1990s,[2] resulting in the creation of the posts of security advisor and risk manager, both at headquarters and in the field. These were, to begin with, filled mainly by former military and police personnel.[3] These experts progressively set up regional coordination platforms[4] and professional networks[5] to develop standards, databases, manuals and training programmes with courses and self-instruction modules designed for all humanitarian workers.[6] Offering training, consultancy services and, in some cases, protection services, specialist companies and NGOs entered the booming humanitarian security market.[7] Private security companies employing veterans from the police, army and intelligence corps (such as the UK's Control Risks Group and France's Amarante) can now boast numerous humanitarian organisations among their clients—Médecins Sans Frontières amongst them.

In the space of twenty years, the dangers inherent in deploying relief operations in conflicts and natural disasters have come increasingly to be treated as risks that can be controlled using methods developed by security specialists. The root of fundamental transformations, this evolution has been considered inevitable, and even positive, by the vast majority of humanitarian organisations, who see it as proof of the growing professionalism of their sector. Backed up by quantitative studies and media news coverage, experts and aid agencies assert that relief workers are now exposed to dangers of unprecedented frequency and nature. Besides the risk of "collateral damage" which one necessarily faces when operating in war zones, they add the threat of being deliberately targeted by criminal or terrorist networks or repressive governments.[8] Given this increased danger, humanitarian organisations appear to have no choice but to professionalise the management of their security by calling on the knowledge and practices developed by experts. They would thus be able to safeguard their operations while fulfilling their moral and legal obligations to their staff, who could potentially sue them for breach of the employer's obligation to protect employees.

Faced with the violent deaths and kidnappings of several of its staff members in recent years in Syria, Central African Republic, the Democratic Republic of Congo and Somalia, some at MSF are also coming to believe that their work environment has become more dangerous. As a result, many association members, from the field to the Board of Directors, are advocating the development of security departments, procedures, training, tools and data collection—and bringing in the know-how of external experts.

The increasing influence of security specialists in humanitarian organisations has, however, elicited numerous questions and criticisms from practitioners and researchers alike. Most critics associate the expansion of security expertise with aid workers being walled off in fortified aid compounds,[9] far not only from danger but from the very people they are supposed to be assisting. Like anthropologist Mark Duffield, criminologist Arnaud Dandoy describes how in Haiti, for example, "in urban areas, as a direct result of the increased sway of the security discourse, humanitarian organisations have retreated behind the walls of fortified residences and offices" and instituted "no-go times" and "no-go zones" for their staff.[10] In Dandoy's opinion, this social and spatial segregation of humanitarian workers reduces their ability to understand their environment and establish relationships of trust with the population and its representatives—which is the only way to create a secure environment conducive to action.[11]

While Médecins Sans Frontières spokespeople regularly condemn the "bunkerisation" of aid agencies and their "risk aversion,"[12] its members privately acknowledge that the association is not always successful in bucking the trend. Moreover, a number of operational managers dispute the reality of the increased danger advanced by the experts to justify the need for their services. Many complain of the mounting pressure they face to report on how they manage security and to apply the best practices recommended in manuals, such as organising and following up on training, creating and updating databases, drawing up crisis management procedures and guidelines, etc.[13] Sometimes doubting the utility of such measures, they often feel obliged to implement them, if for no other reason than to calm the concerns and demands of their boards of directors, management and some field volunteers.

The doubts and controversies surrounding the imposition of security standards, guidelines, indicators and procedures on the workings of humanitarian organisations such as MSF are at the root of this book. How does professionalisation of the security sector help aid workers to cope with the dangers encountered in conflict situations and other crisis settings? Is there an alternative to the dominant security culture? These are the two questions that guide our reflection.

Methodology

This book is divided into three parts. In the first part, we attempt to understand how the debate on security and the role of experts has evolved, both in the humanitarian sector as a whole and within MSF. Bertrand Taithe explores how relief workers have apprehended the notions of risk, danger, security and protection since the nineteenth century while Michaël Neuman relates how the security of teams working in the field has been problematised and debated by MSF-France board members and senior managers since the association's inception.

In the second part, we examine the diagnosis and recommendations made by security risk management specialists. Fabrice Weissman offers an analysis of efforts to quantify violence committed against the aid sector, and, with Monique J. Beerli, provides a study of the security manuals for humanitarian workers published since the latter half of the 1990s.

In the third and final part, we provide an overview of contemporary MSF security practices, using Central African Republic, north Syria and an abduction in the Russian Caucasus as examples. In an interview with Michaël Neuman, Delphine Chedorge describes the responsibilities of a head of mission in charge of security in Central African Republic in 2014. Judith Soussan recounts the security practices implemented by a field team deployed in the thick of the Syrian civil war in an area controlled by a succession of opposition groups (including the Islamic State of Iraq and al-Sham) between 2013 and 2014. In the final chapter, Duncan McLean tells of MSF's controversial efforts to secure the release of a Dutch volunteer abducted in Dagestan in 2002.

The choice of these accounts merits some explanation. Our aim was not to describe the state of MSF's security practices in an exhaustive or representative way, but to shed some light on their diversity and their possible discrepancies with the analytical and action frameworks proposed by security manuals or required by MSF management. We gave preference to what were deemed especially dangerous situations and those that are the focus of current debates on insecurity. The decision to examine a case of abduction was based on the serious impact of kidnappings and the lack of transparency surrounding them. The sometimes debatable legality of the practices used to free hostages, the reluctance of some victims to talk about the harsh conditions of their detention and the fear of making the job easier for future kidnappers by exposing how such cases were resolved combine to enforce a code of silence that is not conducive to analysis and deliberation. This is why we chose to discuss a case from some time ago: namely, the 2002 abduction of Arjan Erkel, the details of which have already been made public in several books and press articles, as well as the legal battle between MSF and the Dutch government.

Before going further, we should make it clear that, strictly speaking, this book does not address the causes of the insecurity affecting humanitarian organisations. While it concludes that it is impossible to establish whether there is a general increase or decline in insecurity, we readily agree that concerns about the perils facing humanitarian teams in many of the areas where they operate are indeed legitimate. Although we discuss on several occasions the type of dangers affecting MSF, we do not aim to provide an exhaustive list of the different situations in which the safety of aid workers is jeopardised. There is a plethora of literature supporting (or debating) the hypothesis that today's humanitarian workers are deliberately targeted due to their lack of independence, impartiality or neutrality. Indeed, a critique of this theory is central to our earlier book, *Humanitarian Negotiations Revealed: The MSF Experience*.[14]

Our deliberations on humanitarian security practices have drawn us to numerous social science texts devoted to the history of risk management in Western societies, the sociology of management tools and the way in which other sectors (military, banks, development agencies, air traffic control organisations, etc.) handle their relationship to danger and uncertainty. In the pages that follow, we will rely on this extensive literature to present the different chapters of our book and propose some answers to the question posed at the beginning of this introduction: how does the dominant security culture help a humanitarian organisation such as MSF to cope with the dangers it encounters in conflict situations and other crisis settings?

How Has the Culture of Security Risk Management Come to Gain Traction?

The End of an Era

In his contribution, historian Bertrand Taithe points out that the notion of risk management was already quite prevalent among the humanitarian foundations and organisations that came into being during the nineteenth century. At that time, it applied to financial and institutional administration of charitable funds, frequently administered by bankers and businessmen anxious to demonstrate their responsible management. Individual exposure to danger in war zones was a completely different story—one of courage and bravery, often recounted in the form of heroic narratives. During the wars of the latter half of the nineteenth century, humanitarian security practices were based on negotiation, the mutual interests of the belligerents and the threat of public denunciation—some going so far as to publish the names of the officers in command of artillery batteries that bombarded hospitals. Although security was rarely what it should have been (far from it), humanitarian narratives often implied the opposite, speaking very little about the great difficulties experienced by those in the field, thereby helping to reinforce the notion that health facilities were neutral, inviolable sanctuaries.

According to Taithe, the paradoxical coexistence of risk management and the spirit of adventure, which persisted through most of the twentieth century, was made possible by the physical distance separating headquarters from the field, unsophisticated bureaucratic procedures and communication systems and the chivalrous spirit of early humanitarian workers. Relief organisation personnel were treated, and saw themselves, as associates of a noble adventure, rather than as employees who might demand of their employers the security guarantees to which fledgling labour law entitled them.

In Taithe's view, the development of a security culture in the aid sector at the turn of the twenty-first century signalled an extension of the risk management approach hitherto limited to the financial administration of charitable institutions. It was, he claims, accompanied by a reconfiguration of the head-quarters–field relationship. Thanks to improved communication systems, and in the name of employee protection, faraway decision-makers began exercising greater control over humanitarian workers, gradually eroding their autonomy and sense of responsibility. This phenomenon was facilitated by a view of the field afforded by remotely transmitted data that allowed headquarters to feel that they were in as good, or even better, a position than the teams to assess the situation and pilot operations. And so the security culture has done away with the fiction and narratives that fuelled the commitment of aid workers. The influence of risk management has led to disenchantment with humanitarian action, whose chivalrous spirit has been drowned in the icy waters of actuarial calculation and remote control.

MSF-France: Calling in the Specialists, Despite the Doubt

Michaël Neuman's study shows that the heroising spirit of chivalry lived on among MSF-France's presidents and administrators until at least the late 1980s. During the association's first twenty years, they considered exposure to danger an essential part of humanitarian engagement, that it conferred a certain nobility. Individual commitment is central to MSF's first charter, whose final paragraph ends on this solemn note: "Anonymous and volunteers, [its members] seek no individual or collective satisfaction from their activities. They understand the risks and dangers of the missions they carry out and make no claim for themselves or their assigns for any form of compensation other than that which the association might be able to afford them."[15] Throughout the 1970s and 1980s, although numerous incidents were already occurring, headquarters had no real control over the day-to-day management of security in the field because of a lack of any direct means of communication.

As Neuman explains, the Board of Directors began viewing insecurity as a problem at the turn of the 1990s when the French section suffered its first violence-related deaths in a context marked by the expansion of relief operations in post-Cold War conflicts. The period coincided with the advent of portable suitcase satellite equipment that was soon replaced by mobile phones. Headquarters began communicating in real-time with field teams, even as bullets were raining down around them. It was then that the organisation issued its "golden rules", framing how risks were to be taken on mission. With the reminder that one "could never count on humanitarian immunity" and that security depended, first and foremost, on understanding the context, positioning and contacts, these "golden rules" imposed three limits on volunteer engagement: the team must not be targeted; it should conduct curative and worthwhile activities; and headquarters took precedence over field in deciding to withdraw.

The interpretation and implementation of these rules were the focus of many debates during Board of Directors and Annual General Meetings throughout the 1990s and early 2000s. Directors would frequently go to the field to meet with the teams and make their own informed judgement, a tradition that was to wane during the 2000s. But there seemed to be agreement on some points: refusal to tolerate deaths and serious injuries occurring on a regular basis, rejection of blanket explanations for insecurity and distrust of the forms that the professionalisation of the security sector was taking.

For the managers of MSF-France, security had been primarily the business of logisticians and project coordinators (and their line managers). Logisticians were responsible for the material aspects of team protection: safe rooms and bomb shelters, transportation and communication equipment, protective equipment, hibernation stocks, evacuation plans, etc. Coordinators, "resourceful and diplomatic", were responsible for the political aspects of security: context analyses, contacts and negotiations, possibly including suspension of activities, withdrawal and public denunciation—the latter having been used as a political tool since the association's beginnings. In the 1990s, in an attempt to defend this logistical and political approach to security, MSF-France leaders refused to create specialist security expert positions or use training courses given by ex-military personnel. MSF did decide, however, to enhance the skills of operational managers in context analysis, in particular via training and the development of research into the relationship between humanitarian action and its political environment. During that same period, expertise in security logistics was formalised, as illustrated by the ever-increasing size of the chapters devoted to security in successive editions of MSF's *Aide à l'organisation d'une mission* guidelines ("Guidelines on Setting Up a Mission").

But risk management culture won in the end. In 2013, after several years of appropriating more and more from specialist training and best practice manuals, MSF-France created the position of "security focal point". How did this change come about?

A More Dangerous World?

The remarkable powers of attraction of risk management are in large part due to a growing sense of insecurity within the aid world over the last twenty years. Yet, as Weissman explains in Chapter 4 of this book, it is impossible to deduce from quantitative studies on violence against aid workers whether the danger is increasing or lessening, or indeed whether aid workers are now targeted for political reasons relating to a perceived lack of independence or neutrality. Figures on humanitarian insecurity are not statistically significant and are used primarily for promotional purposes, to justify the existence and power of a new guild of security professionals[16] and to construct a victim narrative around violence against aid workers, held up as the heroes and martyrs of contemporary wars.

However, according to datasets produced by the Universities of Oslo and Uppsala on armed conflicts, aid agencies have been operating in a world that is no more violent than it was at the end of the Cold War. Indeed, in the 2000s armed conflict killed on average five times fewer people annually than it did in the 1980s, and nine times fewer than in the 1950s.[17] Mass violence against civilians is apparently also on the decline (with the notable exception of 1993 to 1997, which was marked by an exceptional number of deaths in Rwanda and its neighbouring countries).

Although the overall death rate from conflicts is declining, there are obviously episodes of extreme violence with huge human casualties caused by mass killings, famine, and disease. Such has been the case, for example, in Central African Republic, South Sudan and Syria over the past three years, where humanitarian workers regularly face sometimes persistent periods of extreme insecurity.[18]

Furthermore, kidnap now poses a significant risk to aid workers, and for-eigners in general, whatever their occupation. Indeed, the monetary and political value of Western nationals on the international hostage market has been radically inflated by conflicts between armed transnational Salafist groups and states. While the French Ministry of Foreign Affairs stopped announcing in 2009 the numbers of French nationals abducted (or released) in other countries, it did acknowledge that, between 2004 and 2008, the figure had increased from eleven to fifty-nine. During the same period, the number of countries where these abductions took place rose from five to fif-teen.[19] The threat now extends over much of Africa, the Middle East, the Caucasus and Central Asia and, since 2011, there has not been a single year that an MSF section has not seen one of its members disappear or be kidnapped.

In this sense, although attacks against humanitarian workers are no new phenomenon, humanitarian organisations' current concern with security is far from unfounded.

Nevertheless, from the security perspective, the most dramatic change in the past twenty-five years has been the substantial increase in relief operations and the number of humanitarian personnel working in the midst of conflicts. For example, the World Food Programme's staff increased tenfold (from approximately 1,500 to 11,400 permanent employees) between 1995 and 2014[20] and MSF's national and international staff grew from 12,000 in 1998 to 36,500 in 2014. Western governments engaged in containment and stabilisation policies in peripheral conflicts encouraged and financed this increase. As Mark Duffield and others have shown, since the end of the Cold War, Western-led interventions in war-torn or unstable countries have relied heavily on humanitarian organisations to contain crises and population displacements within their own borders and to support peacekeeping and state-building operations.[21]

Normalising Increasing Exposure to Danger

As one might expect, the increase in the number of aid workers deployed to conflict zones and unstable areas has resulted in a greater number of deaths, injuries and kidnappings. The development of risk management in the aid sector appears to be an effort to curb this increase and, in so doing, render occurrences more acceptable according to a logic observed in the history of risk management in Western societies.[22] As historians Jean-Baptiste Fressoz and Dominique Pestre point out, the introduction of the concept of occupational risk in nineteenth-century labour law contributed to both the recognition and the normalisation of the new dangers workers were exposed to as a result of the Industrial Revolution. By treating these unprecedented perils as risks, the legislature made it possible to acknowledge their existence and to make them acceptable, thanks to a system of regulation (standards, indicators, procedures, etc.) and compensation (insurance).[23]

As in other areas,[24] the growth of risk management in the aid sector both recognises and normalises the exposure to danger of large numbers of humanitarian workers now deployed in the heart of conflict zones. This drive for normalisation seems all the more necessary as aid organisations confront the obsolescence of the spirit of sacrifice associated with the ethos of the first generations of humanitarians,[25] a growing social demand for protection[26] and the judicialisation of social relations. In this regard, humanitarian organisations face the same pressures as banks and large corporations, which in the 1990s established formal and auditable risk management mechanisms to protect themselves from lawsuits and scandal in case of adverse events.[27]

Nevertheless, as Michaël Neuman and Jonathan Edwards note in this publication, the risk of legal judgment against an employer for failing to protect an employee is still largely theoretical in the aid sector, though the recent ruling by a court in Oslo, which found the Norwegian Refugee Council guilty of gross negligence in its handling of the kidnapping of Steve Dennis and three other staff members in Dadaab, Kenya in 2012, might change the equation.[28] Yet MSF asks its volunteers and employees to sign contracts with ever more intricate clauses and appendices, to protect the organisation from liability in case of accident. It is also to protect against potential lawsuits that the Boards of Directors of MSF partner sections[29]—legally liable in the event of a lawsuit by one of their section's volunteers on mission—encourage MSF operational centres to adopt the formal risk management measures set out in humanitarian security manuals.

Security in Theory

The Management Approach to Security

First appearing in the 1990s, security manuals were introduced primarily as practical guidelines designed to alert field workers to the dangers they might encounter in war zones. A second generation of manuals, published in the 2000s, called for a managerial approach, with a stated objective of protecting humanitarian organisations from legal and reputational risk. This is the case of the highly influential 'Good Practice Review Number Eight' (GPR 8), published by the Overseas Development Institute (ODI), to which Monique J. Beerli and Fabrice Weissman devote a large portion of their chapter.

At first glance, these manuals look like compilations of recommendations and checklists formalising the know-how developed over time in the field (how to manage communication equipment, organise travel, secure sites, behave in the event of fighting nearby, etc.). Their innovation consists in promoting a "strategic and operational approach to security management" based on detailed calculation, planning and standardised procedures.

The latest manuals intend to replace subjective security assessments with scientific methods to eliminate the biases of human perception. To achieve this, they suggest apprehending risk in its mathematical form (risk = probability [threat, vulnerability] x impact)[30] and refining its calculation using databases. Reminiscent of the actuarial approach adopted by insurance companies,[31] this process tends to disregard the causes and meanings of particular events, in favour of a probabilistic approach relying on mathematical laws to detect risk factors—despite the fact that the events in question (for example, the murder or abduction of an aid worker, an attack on an ambulance or the bombing of a hospital) are far too rare and dissimilar to be modelled using statistical series.

The manuals then recommend defining a "security strategy", preferably relying on a so-called "acceptance" approach. An acceptance strategy aims to cultivate the goodwill of a population and its representatives toward humanitarian workers through a defence of their image as "good people who do good work." In this regard, the GPR 8 describes the press and journalists as a major risk factor: "A poorly worded, inaccurate or inflammatory statement can put staff in direct danger and may even result in expulsion from a country."[32] To contain this risk, standard communication procedures should ensure that everyone in the organisation, from security guard to president, projects the same message—and that no unauthorised documents or statements leak out. Not just their words, but all other forms of humanitarian worker behaviour need to be standardised via codes of conduct and operational procedures to ensure that the intended strategy is correctly applied.

The Ideological Assumptions in Security Manuals

The particularity of second-generation security manuals is not so much that they recommend using rules, indicators and procedures—such regulation mechanisms predate the professionalisation of the security sector and the shift to a "managerial approach". Their innovation is to substantially multiply these tools, and to convey in the guise of technical recommendations the specific ideological assumptions highlighted by Monique J. Beerli and Fabrice Weissman.

First, the GPR 8 and the guidelines modelled on it promote an apolitical view of security challenges. Considering security as a technical problem requiring technical solutions, they obscure the social and political conflicts as well as the power plays and interests that structure the arena where aid agencies negotiate their presence and protection. This apolitical approach is facilitated by the use of the notion of "risk" itself. As sociologist Patrick Peretti-Watel explains, risk is "danger that we consider random, without cause. It is danger for which it is less a matter of blaming culprits for past occurrences than of preventing future occurrences."[33] The apolitical approach is manifest in its recommendations regarding the media—at best considered as merely a means to relay standard marketing campaigns projecting the image of virtuous, consensual humanitarian organisations; at worst, a threat to be neutralised. This distrust vis-à-vis the public sphere contrasts sharply with MSF-France's practices of the 1970s to the 2000s, characterised by repeated public appeals aimed at reinforcing the association's stances in its (often conflict-ridden) dealings with political and military powers capable of affecting its security.[34] In this publication, the account of MSF-Switzerland's efforts to obtain the release of its kidnapped volunteer in the Caucasus is a good example of this.

The manuals' second assumption is the positivism that sees wars and crisis settings as the sum of risks that can be controlled by calculations and planning. Even according to management theories (on which the GPR 8 claims to base its approach), such confidence in the ability of reason to predict and control every possible phenomenon—provided the necessary time, means and expertise are allocated—appears obsolete. For the past fifteen years, authors such as Dominique Genelot have been recommending that businesses base their organisation and management on the notion of "complexity",[35] a term used to designate "anything that is completely or partially outside our understanding or control". The manuals' positivist approach is also at odds with the thinking of military theorists who, following Clausewitz, have considered uncertainty the chief characteristic of the battlefield. Faced with the "fog of war" and the unpredictable behaviour of the military machine, subject to the phenomenon of "friction", many military theorists recommend—as does General Vincent Desportes—using tactical methods based on "trust in man and the flexibility of systems."[36]

Yet the distrust of man is the third assumption conveyed in the latest security manuals. Indeed, they manifest a mistrust that is three-fold. Mistrust of populations that aid agencies are supposed to be helping, but whom manuals tell us to regard as potentially threatening, mistrust of the general public and opinion leaders, considered vectors of risk to reputation, and mistrust of the volunteers themselves. In this last regard, security manuals such as the GPR 8 disregard aid workers' subjective judgement on security, preferring a matrix; they distrust their initiative, preferring standard operational procedures; and lastly, they doubt their loyalty, preferring waivers annexed to their contracts.

The adventurous ethos of the early humanitarians described by Bertrand Taithe—discernible in the notion of the "aristocracy of risk" at MSF—would thus seem to present a particular risk in the eyes of the experts. From the 2000s on, the security manuals contain numerous negative references to "dinosaurs" and "cowboys," and to "adrenaline-addict (...) A-type personnalit[ies]"[37] who are "overconfident that they can handle any security situation because they have been doing it for many years,"[38] when in fact they are throwbacks to a bygone era where "there were fewer threats, [and] greater respect for aid organisations."[39] Their ideal volunteer does not measure the risks and perils of their mission and is not "engaged" with the action. They are docile and responsible; they trust the experts to analyse the risks objectively and to know how they should talk and behave (even as far as in their sex lives) in order to stay safe and protect their comrades and their organisation.

And yet there is a fourth assumption in the manuals: the legitimisation of a rational-legal ethics of sacrifice. According to the GPR 8, "good operational security management" cannot completely eliminate danger or losses. It should, however, ensure that "residual risk" is kept to a minimum via procedures aimed at reducing the probability and impact of incidents, and that such risk is "justified in light of the potential benefit of the project or programme". Danger and sacrifice are acceptable, provided procedures are followed and the cost–benefit ratio is favourable.

The introduction of risk management in humanitarian action is in this way symptomatic of a broader phenomenon, which political scientist Béatrice Hibou terms "neoliberal bureaucratisation:"[40] the invasion of social relations by forms of bureaucratic regulation issuing from the private sector and based on its own abstractions.[41] Hence in the aid world, the concept of actuarial risk is used to apprehend the dangers that humanitarian workers face in war zones and cost–benefit calculations to determine the acceptable level of exposure. The security manuals epitomise this strange mix of neoliberal ideology and technocratic planning fantasy peculiar to many tools of contemporary humanitarian action, such as the widely-used planning and management tool called the "logical framework."[42]

Security in Practice

An approach based on ethnographic observation is needed to accurately describe the practical uses of security tools, procedures, manuals and training and their actual impact on how MSF and similar organisations operate.[43] This is not the aim of the accounts included in this book, as their primary objective is to illustrate the discrepancies between the apolitical, positivist view of danger inherent in risk management and the experience of teams responsible for mission security or securing the release of a hostage. They also offer a glimpse into how the dilemmas created by risk-taking on mission (the subject of the "golden rules" set down in the 1990s) arose, and were resolved, in the situations in question.

The last three chapters of this book begin by describing the broad assortment of dangers that MSF teams face—dangers that cannot be solely attributed to a "lack of neutrality or independence," to paraphrase the dominant interpretation provided in quantitative studies and security manuals. These dangers are associated with the terror strategies used by belligerents: the lynching of enemy wounded inside hospitals by militias in Central African Republic; a machine gun attack on a meeting of prominent citizens inside a hospital; the bombing of hospitals by the Syrian army; the kidnapping, execution and trafficking of hostages by Syrian armed groups; the assassination by these same groups of supposed traitors and apostates among patients and staff; and human trafficking in the Caucasus fuelled by an extremely brutal pacification campaign. But the dangers are also tied to the micro-histories of the missions and the individual behaviours of their members. It might be a social conflict that degenerates into death threats in Central African Republic; or a patient's father who, feeling his son is not getting good care, points his weapon at a doctor in Yemen; or a head of mission who arouses the suspicions of the Russian secret service by acting as a guide for a delegation of American military personnel in the Caucasus.

These studies also show that the risk analyses performed by operational managers are very far from an objective process that neutralises the human factor in favour of mathematical rationality. Understanding of the context and the risks is influenced by the personal paths of heads of mission and project managers, their previous knowledge of the country, their interest in its history and its political actors, and their personal network of relationships. The diversity of personalities and circumstances is reflected in how they obtain information or set up a network of contacts. Some prefer to keep their distance from local society, for fear of being caught up in power struggles between clientelistic networks, while others prefer to create a network of friends who can help them understand the environment and, if need be, actually protect the mission by using their influence or passing on important and well-timed information.

Whatever their approach, operational managers have to handle extremely complex and volatile situations. The last three chapters illustrate the "fog" in which decision-makers must make their decisions, the "friction" associated with the functioning of the MSF machine, and the impossibility of relying on standard procedures when dealing with uncertainties. The limitations of guidelines and training are particularly obvious in the abduction discussed in the book, which underscores the degree to which uncertainty about the kidnappers' identity and motives forced the negotiators to take perilous gambles—which meant disregarding the recommendations of private and government experts. In such uncertainty, profound differences can appear between successive field teams or between field, coordination and headquarters regarding the analysis of the context, the ensuing danger or the usefulness of the mission.

Security is the outcome of constant negotiation with political and military authorities on the choice of activities, the services rendered, the dividing-up of MSF income (salaries and rents), public pressure and the quality of the interpersonal relationships established by operational managers with those around them. We also see the pragmatism of teams that go so far as to delegate some degree of security management to a Salafist politico-military entrepreneur in Syria or to a priest in a Catholic mission in the CAR.

Furthermore, personal freedoms of field volunteers are limited by rules governing their movements and behaviour (dress, attitude, emotional life, etc.), rules created not only for security reasons but also to facilitate human resource management. The accounts show, indirectly, that fear, anxiety, guilt, elation and valuing courage and strength of character play an important role in how aid workers assess risk and the merit of their actions. But they also show that such emotions and merits usually remain unsaid. We see the taboo against certain types of violence that are considered dishonourable—torture and sexual assault, for example—and the lack of transparency between humanitarian organisations (including between MSF sections) about security incidents they experience. This lack of information—like the attitude of project coordinators who feel that they alone are responsible for security—sometimes makes it impossible for field staff to gauge the risks they face in going about their work.

The accounts herein also highlight how difficult it is to interpret the rules (such as the "golden rules") regulating the scope of risk-taking in the field. When the Syrian government bombs hospitals in rebel areas, when jihadist groups declare that "foreign infidel NGOs are not welcome in Syria," or when a Syrian MSF surgeon, known for his militant atheism, is abducted while on call and then killed, is the organisation being targeted? Do MSF's activities in such contexts justify the risk? Opinions differ between, and even within, sections. While activity statistics and efficiency are brought to bear in these debates, the determination of acceptable risk in Syria does not boil down to a cost–benefit calculation and complying with procedures, but includes, among others, the field teams' feeling of "being where they should be." And finally, these accounts underline the ambivalent role of headquarters. By its considerable involvement in security management, depending on the case, it contributes—from the teams' perspective—to over- or underexposing them.

From Bunker to Humanitarian Martyr

The MSF teams mentioned in these studies were not exposed to the "bunkerisation" syndrome described by Arnaud Dandoy and Mark Duffield. We should point out that, unlike the United Nations and many large NGOs, the specialised units dedicated to security at MSF are still in the early stages of their development, and their prerogatives are no greater than those of the Operations Departments, which are still ultimately responsible for the risks that are taken. Yet one cannot help being concerned by the apparently unstoppable spread of the dominant risk management culture. Responding to the need to normalise humanitarian workers' exposure to danger and protect their organisations against legal and reputational risk, it poses a threat to aid workers, holding out a promise of protection that it cannot fulfil while overshadowing the social and political dimensions of their security. And lastly, it drives their organisations towards authoritarianism.

"Bunkerisation" and operational paralysis are only one potential consequence of an ever-expanding risk management culture. At the other extreme, this culture can help render the growing number of dead, wounded and kidnapped acceptable by heroising humanitarian workers while bureaucratically normalising their exposure to danger. This heroisation takes the form of public campaigns aimed at denouncing violence against aid workers while simultaneously contributing to the symbolic representation of humanitarians as heroes and martyrs of contemporary wars.[44] Whether overexposed or overprotected, humanitarian workers tend to be deprived of a sense of engagement in dangerous situations as their employers develop numerous procedures to protect themselves from legal and reputational risk in case of accident.

The alternative to this trend is not to reject, *en bloc*, security indicators and rules. It is to recognise that the dangerous situations in which humanitarian workers operate involve an unavoidable amount of uncertainty, making it necessary to take gambles.[45] The experience of other professionals (such as doctors, fire-fighters or police officers)[46] faced with irreducible levels of uncertainty shows that the more these gambles are based on an empirical analysis of each particular situation (rather than on blanket explanations and general recommendations), the more they rely on practitioners' experience and professional judgement (rather than on the automatic application of routines and formalised procedures), and the more they are subject to deliberation on the means and ends of the actions to be undertaken (rather than to authoritarian, *sub rosa* decisions), the less risky they are. The alternative to the dominant security culture means trusting the practical wisdom of humanitarian workers and helping it flourish by relating and analysing their experiences with danger.

HISTORY

2

ON DANGER, SACRIFICE AND PROFESSIONALISATION

MSF AND THE SECURITY DEBATE

Michaël Neuman[1]

Since its inception, Médecins Sans Frontières (MSF) has confirmed its commitment to working in war zones. Its staff have faced danger, to a greater or lesser degree, throughout the organisation's history. In this chapter we examine how this issue of risk has manifested itself, from the founding of the association[2] to the beginning of the 2010s, notably in discussions during Board of Directors meetings and annual reports presented to the General Assembly. We will see how the debates and deliberations on how best to protect ourselves from danger have been influenced by the growth of MSF, changes in the political context and the advent of "humanitarian security" within the aid system.

The Early Years: The 1970s and 1980s

Romanticisation of Danger and Rejection of Sacrifice

With most of its founding members profoundly marked by their experiences in the 1960s with the Red Cross in Yemen and Biafra (Nigeria), MSF leaders

21

were well aware from the outset of the potential dangers. The confronting of danger in the early years was staged, corresponding to an "aristocracy of risk."[3] This romantic view was reflected in the association's original charter: "Anonymous and volunteers, [its members] seek no individual or collective satisfaction from their activity. They understand the risks and dangers of the missions they carry out."[4]

Referring to the association's Lebanon mission in his 1977 President's Report, Bernard Kouchner paid "special homage to the fifty-six volunteers, men and women, nurses and doctors, surgeons and anaesthetists who, on behalf of Médecins Sans Frontières (MSF), left the tranquillity of France as volunteers to face fear and danger in the name of the brotherhood of human-kind and medical action."[5]

Despite the departure from the organisation in 1979 of many of MSF's founders, Kouchner included, this bravado, in the form of a "heroisation" of the narrative, lived on—but with a rejection of sacrifice. The assertion that "We know there will be a price to pay, because nothing big is ever achieved, nothing gets created or accomplished without risk"[6] was immediately followed by a call for prudence and to heed the advice given by exploratory missions. In 1981, the president agreed: "We are not asked to be heroes, we are asked to do our job, as well as possible, as sincerely as possible, but, above all, to come home."[7]

The 1980s were a decade of very rapid expansion for MSF, both for the French section—whose revenues rose from 7.3 to 207 million francs between 1979 and 1989—and internationally, with the creation of the Belgian (1980), Swiss (1981), Dutch (1984) and Spanish (1986) sections. In 1983–4, MSF-France sent 600 people on mission, almost four times as many as in the mid-1970s.

Moreover, by the end of the 1970s, the association began operating under its own flag in refugee camps, and then, where possible, across borders in countries in conflict: Afghanistan, Honduras, El Salvador, Chad, Sudan, Eritrea and Uganda. Its exposure to risk increased significantly.

In this high-risk environment, the association suffered its first deaths, either accidental or from disease. The first combat-related incidents came in 1980. In Chad, a lone sniper targeted a team of three doctors and wounded one. The same year, in Zimbabwe, a car was machine-gunned, but no one was hurt. In Uganda, where security was non-existent, "a team came close to being massa-cred," but "was only looted."[8] There were also arrests and detentions, some of them lasting months, as in Turkey in 1981.[9] Each incident was considered in isolation, with no wider perspective. MSF was not looking for trends.

In the years that followed, the number of incidents grew, yet there was still no structured response from the organisation. What we now call "security incidents" included teams being caught in aerial bombing raids in Tigray, Ethiopia (1983), a plane carrying volunteers to Mozambique being fired upon (1985) and kidnappings in Chad (Belgian section volunteers in 1984) and Somalia (1987), along with all of the dangers of the Afghanistan mission (bombs, attacks on convoys, etc.). Missions were suspended or evacuated in Sudan, Afghanistan and Mozambique.

The early days of MSF's mission in Uganda, then in the grips of the 1980 famine, illustrate to some extent the improvised and localised approach to security in an extremely dangerous setting, but of which MSF attempted no political analysis. The teams had to contend with criminal acts, primarily committed by livestock traffickers, as well as the unpredictability of soldiers at roadblocks. Their exposure was greatest on the roads and MSF vehicles were sometimes targeted. "We kept our fingers crossed when we came across highway bandits or Tanzanian soldiers. We took the road early in the morning, otherwise soldiers who drank too much would become aggressive and dangerous, and in the towns we drove fast to avoid getting ambushed," recalls Rony Brauman, who was in charge of the mission at the time.[10]

In 1987, with a growing number of humanitarian workers (in Somalia, for example) and journalists (especially in Lebanon) being taken hostage, MSF began wondering whether "a new trend"[11] was emerging. But the president's answer was "no", and there was no change in the narrative on risk-taking.

But while the term "risk management" was almost never used in discussions, a certain consistency in security practices might be remarked upon, characterised by a fledgling professionalism, a high degree of delegation to armed groups, the use of public condemnation and, as a last resort, withdrawal.

Professionalisation, Delegation, Condemnation and Withdrawal

The professionalisation process initiated in the early 1980s stemmed from the will to create a structured and effective organisation: raising funds, developing media contacts, setting up a uniform data collection system and drug lists that were "as consistent and standardised as possible," generalising the use of radio and telex, and using planes to travel when necessary.[12] The position of "coordinator" was created—a role which required both resourcefulness and diplomacy. The association's dread of bureaucratisation was countered with arguments about security and the quality of communications: "We have to stop leaving numerous or widely scattered teams out of contact with France in these dangerous countries."[13] At the time MSF consisted of a very small head office, overseeing missions with which, for lack of resources and technology, it had very limited contact. Information from the field was scarce because it could take days to get to a telephone and letters could take weeks to reach their recipient. In reality, MSF delegated much of its security (and logistics) management to the belligerents, in the belief that they should do their share of the relief work. In Eritrea and Afghanistan, for example, the teams crossed the borders in guerrilla convoys, in a bid to stay safe. This practice remained in use in Angola until the mid-1990s. Such alliances of convenience were not without their difficulties. Logistics did not always follow, communications were erratic, the armed groups could make excessive financial demands and sick volunteers sometimes received poor care. Yet such problems did not cast doubt on either the modus operandi or its legitimacy; this was simply how things were done.

In spite of its rapid growth, MSF was still small and relatively unknown outside France. Meetings with political and military groups in countries where MSF wanted to work were less a time for negotiations than an opportunity to make itself known. MSF's leaders counted mainly on the mobilisation of the public to increase the organisation's influence and extricate itself from dangerous situations. One example was the campaign that publicly condemned the pro-Soviet Afghan government over the detention of Philippe Augoyard, a doctor working with AMI (Aide Médicale Internationale), captured on 16 January 1983 in Logar Province. Another could be found in the denunciation of the Soviet Army's bombing of hospitals run by foreign teams.[14] In 1983–84, together with AMI, MDM (Médecins du Monde) and the FIDH (International Federation for Human Rights), MSF planned to draw up a charter on the protection of medical teams. Ultimately the project was dropped on the grounds that it would have entailed MSF systematically officialising all its activities, which would have been at odds with the organisation's practices and its aspirations to maintain its unofficial status in countries such as Pakistan (used as a rear base for the Afghan mission), Ethiopia's Tigray and Eritrea regions.

The ultimate response to risk was to withdraw. Programmes were suspended in Uganda in 1981 because of safety incidents and again in 1982 in Iran due to widespread insecurity and problems with obtaining access to the population. The decisions to withdraw were made at head office, and in some cases, for example Uganda in July 1981, against the wishes of the field teams.

The Turn of the 1990s: Formalising the Rules, the Drive for Professionalisation and Tensions over Practices

Growth and the End of the Cold War

MSF's French section continued to grow. The number of international volunteer posts increased from 275 in 1990 to 426 in 2000. Head office also expanded, from fifty employees to some 150 during the same period. By the year 2000, MSF had developed into an international organisation with sections in nineteen countries and an increasingly well-established reputation. But, like the rest of the world, it was facing the geopolitical changes brought on by the end of the Cold War.

Withdrawal of Soviet forces from Afghanistan was the first sign of a new era for MSF; in September 1989 it was noted that "the resistance is breaking up."[15] The Mujahideen made it clear to MSF that things had changed: "They no longer feel that the benefit of having humanitarian teams there is worth the price of effectively protecting those teams [...]. The situation is becoming more and more complex; the increasingly acute security problems are difficult to even think about."

As their alliances with "freedom fighters" crumbled, MSF and other humanitarian organisations saw new spaces opening up. In post-Cold War conflicts, as in the wars breaking out in Somalia, Liberia, the former Yugoslavia and the Great Lakes region, it was now possible to work on both sides of the frontline. Under such conditions, the practice of "embedding"—considered a stopgap measure, despite its romantic aspects—was gradually becoming obsolete. In a context marked by a horrific succession of mass crimes, MSF was forced to become more self-reliant in terms of security.

MSF and its First Casualties of War

The increasing number of security incidents made 1988 the "year of living dangerously."[16] And according to President Rony Brauman, it was "only a matter of luck" that no one had been killed. He seemed to anticipate the worst, however, and, by the next General Assembly, he was lamenting the deaths of two volunteers killed when their plane was shot down over southern Sudan in December 1989, and of another who was killed in Afghanistan in April 1990. They were MSF's first casualties of war. MSF-France ceased operations in both countries.

The conflict in Somalia—where, along with Iraqi Kurdistan, the first international military interventions in the name of the protection of humanitarian assistance were launched—ushered in a decade of mass violence and UN interventionism. Countless incidents were reported during meetings of the Board of Directors. Here are just a few examples, to illustrate their variety and impact: "Over the past three months, seven people have been wounded while on mission: three were hit by machine-gun fire by a lone gunman in Mogadishu and four were caught by fire from a helicopter and two light bombers in Sri Lanka," noted the June 1991 President's Report. In October 1991, as a convoy of wounded was being evacuated in Vukovar, Croatia, an MSF vehicle hit an anti-tank mine, which undoubtedly had been planted deliberately. Four people were wounded, one of them seriously. In Liberia, in addition to all sorts of violent incidents, MSF was plagued by large-scale looting, as were all the other aid agencies.

What set the crises in West Africa and the Great Lakes region apart was not only the extreme violence against civilians, as witnessed directly by the teams in Rwanda, Burundi and Zaire from 1993 to 1997, but also the gravity of the security issues. The May 1994 Board of Directors meeting, for example, reported the evacuation of an MSF-Belgium team from Butare, "as the hospital had been emptied of its patients, killed by militiamen, FAR [Armed Forces of Rwanda] and the Presidential Guard,"[17] and some of the Rwandan staff executed. Although there are no precise figures, more than 200 MSF employees were estimated to have been killed between April and June 1994 during the genocide in Rwanda.

The conflict in Chechnya in the Russian Caucasus also caused its share of incidents—notably kidnappings for ransom—and four international staff members of MSF-Belgium and MSF-France were abducted in 1996–97. In June 1997, a Portuguese doctor was assassinated in Baidoa, Somalia. He was the first international staff member to have died from an act of violence since 1990.

Humanitarian Security Concerns Contribute to Structuring the Aid System

As Mark Duffield commented, the increase in MSF's war zone operations was part of "an unprecedented aid industry expansion at every level: geographical reach, funding availability, the agencies involved and the range and complexity of their responsibilities."[18] The deployment of aid workers into the heart of conflict zones considerably increased their exposure. In May 1992, an International Committee of the Red Cross (ICRC) delegate was killed in an explosion in Bosnia, some twenty international workers met their deaths in Burundi during the period 1995–97 and, in December 1996, six ICRC delegates were murdered in cold blood near Grozny in Chechnya. Humanitarian aid observers began to stop seeing these events as "isolated incidents" but as inter-connected. A narrative emerged which acknowledged the danger faced by aid workers in the context of the changing nature of conflicts[19] and the declining status of humanitarian personnel, who were increasingly perceived as being ineffective. Deprived of the ideological and strategic framework of East–West confrontation, wars were now, so the thinking went, driven solely by ethnic or religious resentment and economic predation. Adopting the "new wars" discourse popularised by Mary Kaldor and Paul Collier,[20] many humanitarian actors believed that what characterised these new conflicts was that their primary targets were civilians and those coming to their aid.

Such was the context in which the safety of humanitarian workers made it onto the agenda of international institutions. Take, for example, paragraph 65 of the final communiqué from the June 1997 G8 Summit in Denver, which expressed "grave concern at the recent attacks against refugees as well as against personnel of refugee and humanitarian organizations,"[21] and UN General Assembly Resolution 52/167 on the safety and security of humanitarian personnel adopted in 1997.

The increasing number of security incidents led to a veritable paradigm shift within the aid system as the European Community became a prescriber of security management practices. A European Commission discussion paper on the security of humanitarian workers recommended that institutional donors require partners to demonstrate their ability to assess situations, track and investigate security incidents, establish security guidelines and commit to training and briefing their staff.[22]

Among those promoting "next generation" security management was Koenraad Van Brabant, an anthropologist by training and a researcher at London's Overseas Development Institute (ODI). Van Brabant greatly influenced the professionalisation of security processes. As he pointed out at the time (and in this he was only the harbinger of a growing trend), "...as recent events in Rwanda, Chechnya and elsewhere demonstrate, there is a real need for agencies to invest in acquiring the appropriate security skills."[23] Because, he believed, "assessing risk and determining risk reduction behaviours is a skill that few staff may have, particularly those without professional military training."[24]

All but unanimous in their new geopolitical reading of the period and in seeing the necessity for a fundamental re-think of humanitarian security,[25] humanitarian organisations began recruiting their first security managers. In 1994, the ICRC set up its "security and stress management unit",[26] and the number of humanitarian security initiatives implemented by the aid community soared.[27] The humanitarian security market was booming, fuelled by former military personnel returning to the private sector with the post-Cold War downsizing of Western armed forces.[28]

Formalising the "Golden Rules" and Difficulties Complying With Them

The annual report presented at the 1990 MSF General Assembly included for the first time a section devoted to "security problems", "brought to the forefront of our concerns." It called for a number of measures: smaller missions (to limit exposure); curative mission objectives (inasmuch as exposure must be gauged against a project's medical benefits); more detailed and systematic briefings and regular visits by board members. A sense of the association's collective responsibility began to emerge, as evidenced by the many debates and controversies over security issues in Somalia alone in 1991.

Following attacks in southern Sudan and Afghanistan, in 1990 the operations department established a set of "golden rules".[29] Rather than technical recommendations, these were general principles reiterating part of the framework laid out by the president that same year: understand the context, communicate MSF's work, prioritise curative activities in dangerous environments and "never count on humanitarian immunity". Furthermore, they explicitly reaffirmed head office's authority over the field regarding the decision to withdraw—something that was gradually to take on more meaning as advances in communication technologies afforded MSF managers in Paris increasingly regular contact with their missions. The year 1992 saw an all-important addition to the golden rules which established a red line whereby any team being specifically targeted must be withdrawn.

Concerned by this change in the nature of their responsibilities, and reckoning that they regularly violated the withdrawal-if-targeted rule, the programme managers made known their disquiet to the Board of Directors. Meanwhile, militias in Somalia were targeting infrastructure and aid workers and MSF recruited armed guards to ensure their security. This was a shift from earlier practices in Afghanistan, Eritrea and Angola as the *de facto* political authorities no longer provided protection. MSF teams—now managing small military units—saw their position weakening in negotiations with this new breed of employee. Despite extremely heated debates both before and during the deployment of armed guards, the decision to continue the Somalia mission won out, "given its practical utility" and the lack of "alternative solutions."[30]

Equally controversial was the decision not to pull out the teams from Burundi in the second half of the 1990s. In 1995–96, the number of attacks and threats against humanitarian agencies escalated in the country.[31] The situation was dire, as massacres were occurring not far from MSF teams, frustrated by their inability to provide assistance, and missions lived from one evacuation to the next. The Board of Directors held numerous discussions on the question of the risk to staff and whether to continue activities. At a June 1996 meeting, right after the assassination of three ICRC delegates, someone asked, "Why must we stay when seventeen foreigners have already been killed?"[32] To the question of whether the activities warranted the taking of such high risks, the operations director answered that it was sometimes necessary to take risks even when one was not treating "a lot of people."[33] On the other hand, the deputy operations director responsible for emergency missions said he "couldn't imagine [himself] briefing someone to go to Burundi."[34] Why were people being killed, they pondered? Was it because of where they were, or because they were humanitarian workers? The debates provided no satisfactory answers to these questions.

Those in favour of staying put advanced two arguments: the scope of the population's needs and the teams' willingness to continue their work. The communications director, himself a former programme manager, took the operations director to task, criticising her "sacrificial" approach. She, in turn, went on to encounter someone even more "sacrificial" when, on a visit to Burundi, she attempted to withdraw the teams from the north against the head of mission's advice. She had to inform the departing teams herself, "because the Human Resources people no longer wanted to do it."[35]

During the Board of Directors meeting in June 1996, President Philippe Biberson argued for staying: "All this addresses a real need, and leaving would mean abandoning people."[36] The Board members voted eleven to four in favour of Operations' decision to keep the team in the field—subject to the team's agreement. Although the decision was ultimately taken not to pull out, at times the association appeared to be feeling its way forward in the dark, with no roadmap to guide it.

The "golden rule" on being targeted was thus shattered in Burundi. Programme managers there had for some time viewed it as inadequate, given the high degree of exposure—especially in the case of projects where humanitarian workers were subject to direct attack on a regular basis.[37] In fact, teams were often kept in place even when field missions were embroiled in recurring violence, including in situations where it would have been impossible to get them out, such as Kigali in Rwanda during the spring of 1994 or Sierra Leone's Freetown in the winter of 1998. However, what was striking in those chaotic times was the intensity of the discussions and the involvement of the Board members, some of whom monitored missions, conducted field visits (for example, in Somalia and Yugoslavia) and shared their analyses on their return.

Resistance to Professionalisation

As an organisation that had defined professionalisation as an historical necessity,[38] MSF might have been expected to embrace technological and bureaucratic advances in security—especially given that, in the mid-1990s, it supported more than it challenged the normalisation and professionalisation process that had accelerated significantly within the aid sector since the African Great Lakes crises. Despite strong pressure to change its practices, however, the association attempted to resist the increasingly technological and professional direction that humanitarian security was taking. In 1991, President Rony Brauman had underlined "the limitations of a global discussion on security"[39] and, two years later, expressed his scepticism toward the "rather approximate reports on the closing off of the world and a new international context where humanitarian action is becoming more and more difficult and less and less accepted."[40]

MSF could not escape the discourse of "new wars", and many felt that it was a different—and more dangerous—world. But the association's leaders voiced their distrust of the trend toward professionalised security. "The most talked about subject after the humanitarian blues is the security of humanitarian workers! Some organisations are offering their volunteers (can we still call them volunteers?) security training—what to do when you're taken hostage—by retired military personnel hired as security experts. Some NGOs actually advocate sharing information and communication networks in sensitive areas with official intelligence agencies!"[41] fulminated in 1998 President Philippe Biberson, an advocate of MSF maintaining its own security management approach.

Analyses became more formalised with the creation in 1995 of MSF's Centre de Réflexion, which published research into major crises—the *Populations in Danger* series—and contributed to coordinators' training. "Environment Week," first held in 1995, was not a technical training course, but was devoted to analysing the aid agencies' environment (hence its name), the political dynamics of conflicts—an understanding of which is essential to operations management—and security. The Board of Directors had a specific place for "qualified, well-known figures" such as Jean-Christophe Rufin and political analyst Guy Hermet.

At the same time, the importance of protective measures and their reinforcement—such as calling in experts in the case of kidnappings—was discussed regularly.[42] There was no shortage of security procedures, quite the opposite in fact. The security chapters in successive editions (1990, 1994 and 2003) of *Aide à l'organisation d'une mission* (Guidelines for Setting Up a Mission) were full of them. They talked about the importance of ensuring that employees and equipment be clearly identified with the MSF logo, the "essential" role of the radio and the need to prepare an evacuation plan. Programme managers were sometimes alarmed at how insulated the teams were becoming and by "the walls and the barbed wire that were going up" around living and work places, without the context seeming to justify it.[43]

Terror and the Temptations of Exceptionalism and Bureaucracy

Mounting Fear

The 2000s were marked by sustained growth for humanitarian organisations, in terms of both resources and ambitions, due in particular to the Afghanistan and Iraq invasions and the considerable humanitarian funding that accompanied them.[44] Yet it was during those years of growth that the narrative of the narrowing humanitarian space and increasing dangers to staff escalated.[45] The deadly strikes in 2003 on the UN and ICRC headquarters in Baghdad were considered emblematic of an unprecedented rise in deliberate attacks against humanitarian workers. Fear was being fuelled by the difficulties facing relief organisations in the Middle East and Sahel, due to the expansion of radical jihadist groups and repeated kidnappings for ransom. While in the 1990s the upsurge in attacks against humanitarian workers was associated with the deliberate targeting of civilians in conflict situations, a view emerged at the turn of the 2000s condemning the targeting of humanitarians as such.

To use the words of Larissa Fast,[46] a narrative of "humanitarian exceptionalism" was being constructed, portraying humanitarian workers as heroes and martyrs. One specific illustration was the designation of 19 August—the anniversary of the attack on the United Nations in Baghdad—as World Humanitarian Day to honour "those who face danger and adversity in order to help others."[47] Statistics would prove a powerful ally in this victimisation device. Starting in the early 2000s, relief and research organisations conducted numerous quantitative studies on violence against humanitarian workers, all of them concluding that increasing insecurity was a scientifically established fact.[48]

Educational institutions began offering degrees in security management. In 2000, the ODI published authoritative guidelines entitled "Operational Security Management in Violent Environments," in which author Koenraad Van Brabant devoted 350 pages to defining good humanitarian security practice.[49] In December 2004, the UN created the Department of Safety and Security (UNDSS) with, as its first director, a former senior Scotland Yard officer. The trend toward professionalisation was justified, not only by "new threats", but also by the need for humanitarian organisations to meet their legal obligations as employers.

In the 2000s, Médecins Sans Frontières was also experiencing steady growth. The budgets for its missions rose from €59 million in 1998 to €219 million in 2010, with 600 international field posts that year compared to only 400 ten years earlier. From 1996 to 2012, the number of national staff under contract grew from approximately 3,000 to more than 5,500.

Those growth years were also years of grief and anxiety for MSF as the organisation suffered a series of assassinations and kidnappings. In July 2000, a French volunteer was abducted in Colombia and held for six months and, in 2001, MSF-Holland's head of mission in Chechnya was also abducted and released some weeks later. In August 2002, the head of the Swiss section's mission in Dagestan was kidnapped.[50] Held for almost two years, his release caused a public dispute between MSF and the Dutch government, which took the organisation to court to demand payment of the ransom it claimed to have paid. Between 2004 and 2008, six international staff members were assassinated while on mission. Five members of the Dutch section, including two Afghanis, were executed in June 2004 in Afghanistan's Badghis Province and an MSF-France logistician died in 2007 when her vehicle was ambushed in Central African Republic. The following year, two international staff members of MSF-Holland and their Somali colleague were killed when their car was hit by an exploding roadside bomb in Kismayo in Somalia.

Those events lent credence to victim discourse and statistics on the worsening security situation, which were echoed by MSF. "It is very important to remember that between 2000 and 2005, 271 international humanitarian workers were killed, [and that] the number of high-risk situations, hold-ups, abductions and physical attacks experienced by our teams continues to grow," lamented in 2006 the Boards of MSF-France and its partner sections (MSF-USA, MSF-Australia and MSF-Japan), who were becoming increasingly involved in decisions on the conduct of the social mission. Indeed, the internationalisation of MSF also contributed to the rise in security concerns. In 2006, the partner sections became responsible for paying their national personnel, who had previously been under contract to MSF-France. More employers meant more legislative frameworks governing their legal liability ("duty of care")[51] for personnel security. In response to this increasing legal pressure, the contracting sections sharpened their requirements.

Such was the background for debates at General Assemblies and meetings of the Board of Directors, which were dominated by at least three issues: the persistent unease created by the discrepancies between the rules instituted in the early 1990s and what was actually happening in the field, the role of head office and the Board of Directors in evaluating risk and making decisions and the legitimacy of transferring risk to national staff or to nationalities at lower risk.

Were the "Golden Rules" Obsolete?[52]

What was the explanation for the attacks against MSF and the ICRC, particularly in Iraq and Afghanistan? A source of concern to MSF leaders was the use of humanitarian rhetoric by Western powers that created a "deadly confusion" between NGOs and foreign armed forces. This was especially the case in Iraq and Afghanistan, and even more so after the Taliban claimed responsibility for murdering five MSF members in Afghanistan's Badghis Province in June 2004, accusing MSF of "work[ing] for American interests."[53] Yet the President's Report for the year 2000 reveals the critical distance that Philippe Biberson wanted to maintain from a narrative blaming such confusion for all of the danger: "If NGOs team up with the military, then they will logically be considered a party to the conflict and targeted or prohibited from staying. [...] But we can also come up with loads of situations where our security depends on what people imagine our political sympathies to be and on the number of guards around us. In reality, and since time immemorial, it is not independence that conditions access to victims, or even the safety of our teams. Most often, it is negotiation (and logistics...)."[54]

However, what seemed to be worrying the association was that "extremist groups have clearly stated that humanitarian workers would be targeted" in Afghanistan and Iraq.[55] During the Board of Directors meeting following the

2003 assassination of an ICRC representative in Uruzgan in Afghanistan, association president Jean-Hervé Bradol expressed his concern at "having to do briefings where we have to warn departing volunteers that there are people who have it in for us," adding that "ten years ago, it was clear to us that this was the red line that would make us give up."[56] "We have no desire to be martyrs to the humanitarian cause, it would be absurd," he continued a few months later.[57]

In this he was following in his predecessors' footsteps. He recognised that the conflict between what was being said and what was being done had to be elucidated. Yet, as we have seen, that conflict already existed back in the 1990s.[58] As the entire MSF movement was in the midst of heated debate over the future of activities in Iraq at the time of the US invasion of the country, Bradol confirmed: "The truth about our current risk exposure policy is that it seems to assume that people are being killed or seriously injured on a regular basis."[59] He challenged this shift all the more since in his view what it achieved was not justified by the operational results. Hence, it was precisely because he believed in the usefulness of delivering aid in Baghdad when the US invaded Iraq that he supported keeping teams on the ground. He was outraged that those opposed to his thinking could suspect him of wanting to deploy teams "simply in the name of an ideal"—"We send teams in when we believe concrete assistance can be provided, which is the case in war-torn towns and cities".[60] After the killings in Badghis in Afghanistan, he criticised "poorly thought-out, oversized" operations.[61]

Trust Procedures and Be Wary of People?

These questions prompted a new round of discussions about the respective roles of the head office, the Board of Directors and field volunteers in taking risks. At a Board of Directors meeting on Central African Republic a little more than a year after the death of a volunteer logistician there, the programme manager asked that the directors collectively assume mission-related risks and make a greater contribution to operational discussions.[62] The following year, when the issue of directors' participation in discussions on security came up again, a member of the management team (who had been operations director from 1986 to 1998) recalled "administrators visiting the missions in an effort to bring a fresh (but not inexperienced) eye. They asked naive questions, sometimes painful, and then they went back to report to the other directors, to share and have exchanges with the field."[63] It is hard not to see this comment as barely veiled criticism of administrators less involved than some of their predecessors in the 1990s.

Successive presidents cautioned everyone against the importance being accorded to procedures and the tendency to centralise decision-making at head office, to the detriment of individual judgment, despite the fact that "the most important protection is our positioning, our understanding of the context and our ability to establish relationships." From that perspective, it was emphasised, "the Board of Directors is more inclined to trust in people, rather than a system and procedures, to make decisions."[64]

In his final President's Report in 2008, Jean-Hervé Bradol distinguished between the responsibilities of the association—to ensure that there is "a certain type of efficacy of action" and that "particular attention is paid to the misappropriation of our resources," and to draw the line when "a political group that could relatively realistically put its threats into action announces that it intends to target humanitarian workers and assassinate them"—and the decision of each individual on exposing themselves to risk.

"Remote Control" and "Profiling"

In more and more settings, "trust in people" means trusting in national personnel, to whom the day-to-day management of activities is delegated, while international managers visit as often as possible. This operating mode—known in humanitarian parlance as "remote control" and often considered a major compromise and downgrade of the conventional method of interventions—was the price MSF had to pay to continue working in places such as the Russian Caucasus and later Somalia. Remote control raises questions about the status of national staff (are they MSF, like the others?) and the specific risks that their involvement in the situation, be it their social, emotional or political ties, might lead them to take.

The setting up of remote control coincided with a discussion on the place and role of national staff that went far beyond the issue of security. Under discussion was a proactive policy intended to raise the status of national employees through better remuneration and access to expatriation, training and association membership. It should be noted that MSF only started keeping records of its local employees in 1994, and, except for a few anecdotal cases, it would take the organisation almost another ten years to seriously take account of their security. These concerns came to a head a few years later as expressed by President Marie-Pierre Allié in 2009: "[W]e should be thinking about the risks our staff are taking. It seems to me that, when we have only national staff in the field, we don't take into account something very specific:

that their personal involvement with the local population may push them to take greater risks than we would wish for them. We should be careful not to underestimate the risks they take."[65]

The growth of radical Islamic groups—notably with the emergence of Al-Shabaab in Somalia and Al-Qaeda's mounting influence in the Maghreb and Arabian Peninsula—contributed to more heated debate on the threat of kidnap and "profiling"; that is, recruiting volunteers based on their gender, religion, nationality or skin colour. Thus, it was explained, given that certain profiles are less exposed, "MSF might consider choosing international staff 'compatible' with the situation, for example, by 'Africanising' teams working in the Sahel."[66] Far from considering withdrawal an option—except in situations where the association is directly faced with the death of its international volunteers, like in Somalia and Afghanistan—MSF views the adjustments to its modus operandi as a pragmatic response to allow it to continue to work in settings where it is highly exposed.

The technical and procedural components of security are expanding and becoming increasingly centralised. While it is difficult to determine objectively what the dangers are and whether they are worsening, it is an established fact that fear—as a social construct—is mounting. The fear of abduction looms particularly large in MSF's attention to what it now labels "highly insecure environments". In light of this, the use of technology may appear to be a solution that reassures. The 2003 edition of *Aide à l'organisation logistique d'une mission* makes the logistics coordinator responsible for "limiting the risks taken by the teams through ensuring that the means and methods implemented for security are present, reliable and correctly used," thus testifying to the increasingly compartmentalised and technology-dependent nature of security management in the missions. In the early 2010s, the operations director recognised "the pressure to professionalise security management."[67] Expressions adopted from leading publications in the sector—such as "risk analysis" or the "acceptance, protection and deterrence" security triangle—are coming into widespread use in MSF's missions and ever-increasing in-house security training courses. Previously unwilling to appoint a "security focal point", the French section—which had been an exception, including within the MSF movement—finally yielded in 2013.

3

DANGER, RISK, SECURITY AND PROTECTION

CONCEPTS AT THE HEART OF THE HISTORY
OF HUMANITARIAN AID

Bertrand Taithe[1]

The concepts of danger, risk, security and protection—none of which are self-evident or simply observable realities—require a broad historical frame to make sense of their meanings in current debates. They have been borrowed, shaped and reinvented in the discharging of humanitarian policies as ways of engaging with aid work. Humanitarians have consistently made their deployment in the face of danger a badge of honour (this use of a nineteenth century notion is deliberate, as it conveys the origins of numerous contemporary issues). In the face of danger, while taking risks, aid workers have always paid attention to their security and sought to define how their work could be made safer, often combining practical measures on the ground with more discursive claims to provide and obtain protection for and through their work.

Yet the evidence shows that in some acutely violent places security was at times minimal or indeed almost non-existent and humanitarians' demands for protection were flouted. Evaluation and management of risk to establish security measures as well as calls for protection turned out to be, for the historian, essential tools for representing and comprehending, not only the world in which humanitarians work, but also the humanitarians themselves.

This chapter comprises three parts. The first provides a brief history of the tools at the centre of risk and protection measures, the second, a longer view of the relationship between security and protection, and the third, how the two concepts have been set, since the 1990s, as a dialectic challenge to humanitarians. It concludes with a reflection on how these concepts have reshaped the notion of the "humanitarian field" in relation to humanitarian work.

Evaluations and Risk

The Legal and Insurance Thinking Behind "Risk"

Humanitarian aid was for the most part deployed throughout the nineteenth century to mitigate the consequences of disasters and industrial accidents, principally fires, shipwrecks, floods and mining disasters. The notion of risk is closely linked to that history, on several accounts. The concept of risk assessment stems from the legal and insurance policy language adopted in the mid-nineteenth century, when the term was adopted by loss adjusters and actuaries whose task it was to anticipate the full extent of risk-taking, even in dangerous but nevertheless insurable occupations.[2] Their main challenge was to establish who was taking the risk and to what extent exposure to danger represented evidence of negligence. Was danger preventable and, if so, by whom and in what timeframe? Was an employee taking a risk a wilful or negligent act? Did people step unknowingly into the path of danger?

These rather obscure points of law are of importance to the humanitarian sector on two levels. Firstly, the history of risk in the wider social context is rooted in the history of legal as well as insurance policy thinking (including social insurance policies), and secondly, the manner in which humanitarians and organisations think about danger relates to the legal history of accidents and criminal negligence trials.[3]

There are numerous examples of a voluntary compensation culture whereby funds were raised to compensate the losses of innocent victims and rebuild the lives of survivors, providing the model for reconstruction and rehabilitation relief in times of war. In 1871, the English Quakers decided to disregard soldiers (even though they were viewed as the primary humanitarian subjects) to focus instead on rebuilding civilian lives after the ravages of the Franco-Prussian War.[4] Like other humanitarian workers in the United Kingdom, they did not venture unequipped into the field and, similar to most voluntary societies or relief funds, they relied on evidence drawn up by accountants. They were particularly dependent on reports compiled by the actuary, a new profession in accountancy. Actuarial reports were specifically designed to provide "scientifically" grounded evaluations of financial liability and measure financial risk to ensure effective and accountable management of relief funds raised for a specific purpose. The term "security" in this economic model referred to the assets held against such risk.[5] Funds committed to relieve the sufferings of widows and orphans had to serve over the long-term because they were pledged to provide until the natural death of the beneficiaries. Consequently, the long lives of beneficiaries were viewed as a risk to the fund. A further risk, a sort of "moral hazard", emerged when the funds were deemed to be too generous as, in the nineteenth century, providing relief was to run the risk of fostering dependency and through dependency to create unlimited liability.[6] Charities were therefore keen to provide enough for long enough, but not too generously. Combined with legal requirements, these moral and practical financial considerations defined risk.

Security issues were to be understood in relation to those arising from limited or unlimited liability. In Anglo-American common law, the codification of danger is related to the notion of peril.[7] In many ways this term defined the concept of preventable danger, the responsibility of individuals in relation to each other and the relative degree of negligence of each party involved in an accident. In the case of accidents, the original "doctrine" of "last clear chance" defined the responsibility of one negligent party towards another as the responsibility of an individual to assist a person in danger if at all possible (without incurring excessive risk) or if the danger could have been foreseen.[8] The legal obligation to intervene in order to prevent harm was defined in court primarily as a duty to assist those in peril.[9] In many respects, these legal concerns (the French "*non-assistance à personne en danger*")[10] related closely to the origins of humanitarianism that merely extended their remit—but not their legal framework—to the global stage.

If the notion of danger and obligation to intervene were thus established early on in Roman and common law, the relationship and unnecessary exposure to danger have a rather more complex and controversial history. Known as the "humanitarian doctrine",[11] a new concept emerged in the early twentieth century in Anglo-American common law which established that to take risk needlessly was not necessarily an admission of full responsibility. In other words, when a person puts themselves in danger out of negligence and the danger itself was created by the negligence of others (typically a moving vehicle or an industrial accident), the two negligent acts do not cancel each other out and the victim might still seek redress or compensation. In humanitarian doctrine, the negligent party at the origin of the danger to which other negligent parties would subsequently expose themselves was still the source of the accident. In practice, this meant that careless employees exposed to unnecessary risks by their employers could still seek legal redress against them. In medicine, the notion of risk was often raised in relation to insanity and the danger a patient might present to themselves or others, making risk assessments a common prerequisite for internment in secure hospitals.

Humanitarian efforts of the late nineteenth century and the contemporary humanitarian matrix originated from this capitalistic social context. The logic and structure of these early efforts were in line with the practices of their promoters.

Risk Exposure: From Insurance to Humanitarianism

The founders of Western humanitarian aid—such as the bankers and lawyers of Geneva, or, in the British Empire, Lord Sutherland and his Stafford House Committee—used a language and logic acquired from their legal and financial practices.[12] They were applying their professional standards to the management of resources mobilised for humanitarian relief. The humanitarians responsible for dispatching medical relief to France during the Franco-Prussian War in 1870–1871, the Ottoman Empire in 1878 and South Africa during the 1899–1902 Boer War adopted the same cautious approach as they would for their own investments. For example, the administrator of the Stafford House Committee, which raised resources for a wide range of humanitarian operations and ran field hospitals during the 1877–1878 Russo-Turkish War, demonstrated full accountability, precision, prudence and responsibility.

In practice, this meant that the Committee, which in 1877–1878 funded fifty medical staff, maintained twenty hospitals, handled three evacuations by train and treated over 75,000 surgical cases, exercised careful management of its funds while appraising the nature of its work, the duration of its operations and its exit strategy according to the rules of risk management.[13] One of the most important risks for the Committee was its image and the fund's reputation. Notably, it had to fend off allegations of corruption that arose from working too closely with Ottoman politicians.[14]

Yet this language of prudence was also melded with recognition of the dangers and risks inherent to war. The two were perfectly compatible because intervening during a war was not expected to be without danger. In many respects, perils and dangers belonged to a different semantic and cultural register, highlighting and valuing danger as an opportunity to reveal individual valour, masculinity, compassion and character. This language of danger was to be found in travel narratives often recounting the risks taken by travellers, missionaries and vicarious humanitarians and their overcoming of danger. The figure of the heroic explorer standing alone in the face of great danger is significant among the humanitarian leaders of the late nineteenth century— from Dr Livingstone to General Gordon[15] or the more controversial Roger Casement.[16] In the twentieth century, polar explorer Fridtjof Nansen, who embodied the humanitarian agenda of the League of Nations, was himself an adventurer in the same noble tradition of danger-seeking individuals.[17]

This relationship between travel narratives, heroics and humanitarian aid has not entirely disappeared. I came across this respect for the skills of the traveller during a recent interview with Jacques Pinel, the pioneer of logistics at MSF, when he informed me that, in the early days, he primarily recruited experienced and adventure-seeking globetrotters and backpackers, the so-called 'routards', as logisticians.[18]

Some of the field experience so prized in humanitarian circles is still expressed through rhetorical tropes and sometimes tones of orientalism dating back to the late nineteenth century. Courage is, to this day, a highly valued humanitarian virtue. It is not surprising then that many of the humanitarian ego-narratives emerging from this period were framed as "adventures".[19] In the dry language of reports and in first-hand accounts, humanitarians would highlight danger in self-reinforcing terms, often dictating a new economy of relief and practice. As Rebecca Gill[20] has shown and I myself have explored,[21] this language of emotive engagement was compatible in practice (although not in discourse) with the "cold calculation" and reasoned action called for by Henry Dunant in his *A Memory of Solferino*.[22]

Yet such reasoning was by no means precise. While by the 1880s it was fairly well established what the statistical chances were that a miner's widow might live to the age of seventy, estimating the chances of being killed in a war was still a somewhat inexact science. Calculating the precise number of war victims was no less straightforward. The discursive work of Jean-Charles Chenu, the French statistician involved at the origins of the French Red Cross,[23] illustrated how war itself remained a largely unknown quantity. For instance, as the Crimean War (1853–1856) was fought (on land at least) on a peninsula accessible only by ship, it should have been relatively easy for the authorities to calculate casualty numbers, given that they knew how many soldiers had been sent in and how many returned. But it would take them over three years to produce detailed statistical accounts and narratives. Still today, war casualty accounting is a source of debate and controversy. Even in times of open warfare, it is no easy task to classify exactly what is the result of direct violence rather than accident, what destruction takes place by design rather than so-called "collateral damage".

Humanitarian concerns reshaped the perception of war, not simply as danger faced in battle but also, and often predominantly, as biohazard. Evidence shows that during the pre-World War One era humanitarian workers were far more likely to succumb to diseases contracted by soldiers and refugees than to physical violence. The nature of that risk remained framed within the medical literature. Yet biosecurity was already a major concern, with early Pasteurian medicine's vaccines offering only limited protection. The risks to surgeons and health workers during surgery were extremely high in the early days of modern humanitarian aid (so-called hospital rot, septicaemia, blood poisoning and other forms of cross-contamination). They undoubtedly lessened during the twentieth century, thanks to new standards in cleanliness and asepsis, but the risk of becoming contaminated during typhus, typhoid, cholera and plague epidemics remained real until the 1940s. In the 1870s, a substantial percentage of medical staff would fall ill and some would die in any humanitarian operation involving large numbers of civilians and soldiers. For instance, by the end of June 1878, one-third of the thirty-nine medical staff serving directly under the responsibility of Stafford House Committee manager Barrington Kennett had been taken ill with typhus; two died of the disease, but none from the conflict.[24] By historical standards, Ebola and the risks it poses to aid workers would appear to be more of a throwback to the past than the emergence of a new category of humanitarian risk.

Security and Protection

Humanitarian Sanctity?

The historical relationship between medical humanitarian aid and wartime 'secours aux blessés'[25] (as the original name of the Red Cross originally entailed) requires looking back at history to consider how notions of "security", "danger" and "risk" were encoded and used and how humanitarians, who have always been working under fire, related to those notions to make sense of their practices and cope, individually as well as collectively.

The 1870–1871 Franco-Prussian War provides instances of the enhanced status afforded to hospitals as sanctuaries and the repeated violations of this status. The right of sanctuary constituted a form of protection in as much as the Red Cross emblem signalled an international healthcare space in the midst of war. Part of the moral apparatus of the Geneva system, this implicit internationalisation of conflicts remains to this day. Yet the use of the emblem was prone to abuses and sanctuary to violation. In 1870, German authorities accused the French public of abusing the system by claiming right of sanctuary for individual houses converted into makeshift ambulances, for example in Le Mans. A house protected by the Red Cross emblem could not be billeted with enemy soldiers, but Germans objected to "hospitals" which contained only one or two wounded soldiers. French authorities accused the German high command of shelling hospitals despite the legal protection afforded by the Red Cross flag.[26] Throughout the 1877–1878 Russo-Turkish War, field hospitals funded by the Stafford House Committee witnessed numerous violations of the Geneva Convention. In January 1878, the hospital where Drs Beresford and Stiven were working in Rustchuk (now the city of Ruse in Bulgaria) was systematically shelled:

> There was no doubting now the intention of the Russians as regarded our hospital, as shell after shell fell in our vicinity while we were busily engaged in placing the patients under the protection of the centre wall of the first ward. So great was the panic caused by the first three shells that were fired, that all the patients that were able to walk took flight in the open plain, where the snow is at present lying over three feet deep, and not only they but all the domestics and other officers of the hospital, so that Dr Beresford and myself were quite alone with some 80 patients to do what best we could for their safety. We went to our work, nevertheless, and lifted the patients in our arms and placed them on mattresses under the wall... The Russians kept on firing till sunset up to which time they had fired between 30 and 40 shells at our hospital, eight of which entered into the different wards of the hospital.[27]

Stiven handed over to the British press the names of the Russian batteries guilty of the transgression (Menschikoff and Esmurda) along with those of the officers in charge in an attempt to name and shame and bring about some symbolic redress. Similar anecdotes exist for all conflicts since 1870, confirming the lack of substance behind claims of sanctuary or, at the very least, their contested status in the midst of fast-moving tactical war operations.[28]

In reality, negotiating neutrality and the use of recognisable emblems were never that straightforward. As a general rule, conspicuous respect for humanitarian neutrality has always been part of a wider strategic master plan, based on reciprocity and/or on the need to establish the legitimacy of the combatant parties. It was undoubtedly a significant propaganda victory for a new world power when the Japanese army received praise for its admirable treatment of Russian prisoners in 1904–1905.[29]

These tools of negotiation were key, particularly when the parties involved made their claims to sovereignty via the protection and responsibilities for delivery of humanitarian aid. One of the key outcomes of early twentieth-century wars was the embedding of humanitarian relief as an auxiliary of recognised military health hierarchies and structures. Humanitarians regularly wore special uniforms and took on specific social roles, which, while civilian in nature, were associated with treating the wounded, the good handling of prisoners and even the rituals around the disposing of corpses following wars or natural disasters in China.[30] The trade-off for these roles was the safety and neutrality granted to medical staff, despite their proximity to the military. But revolutionary and insurrectional warfare granted no such privilege. Civil wars provide many instances of violations of the neutrality of casualties and challenges to the concept of humanitarian sanctuary. Humanitarians themselves often took sides, rejecting any notion that their work should be neutral. Volunteers to the American Medical Bureau Field Unit in the Abraham Lincoln Brigade were explicitly adjuncts to the International Brigade movement during the Spanish Civil War in the 1930s.[31] Nevertheless, in conventional conflicts, a person could be partisan and still claim Genevan neutrality. During the Russo-Turkish conflict these humanitarians' predecessors were able to claim neutrality (largely in vain) under the Geneva Convention, despite the fact that they only assisted Ottoman soldiers and subjects. But there was even less hope of the principles of the Convention being evoked with any success in the case of an extremely cruel civil war. In the Spanish context, risk-taking was often portrayed as the nature of the engagement of volunteers and a testament to the solidarity of non-combatant forces with fighting units.

Risk-Taking Humanitarians

While danger and risk affect individuals differently, the impact on organisations is far more consistent. An organisation cannot be brave, only its members can, and safety was always a concern for those kept at arms-length from danger. Even in the earliest accounts of danger recounted using the most heroic language, organisations and their administrators alike sought to negotiate the safe passage of humanitarian practitioners. In most cases, their safety was entrusted to third parties (who could be called "brokers" or "gatekeepers"),[32] government and local figures of authority. While "characteristics of courage, devotion and endurance"[33] remained paramount, they were unfailingly framed within a context of alleviated risk.

The nature of humanitarian work and the conditions in which it was, and still is, practiced often confronted workers with exceptional forms of suffering and posed new personal risks. The notion of risk to self was always of fundamental concern. While the first 1864 Geneva Convention pre-dated the "psychological turn" of the late nineteenth century, danger in the battlefield had to be understood fairly broadly, since both overwork and excessive compassion could become forms of risk. Indeed, the first instance of burn-out in humanitarian context is depicted by Dunant, who portrayed it as the character failing of a sentimental do-gooder. Primarily originating in accidents—railway in particular—the late Victorian notion of trauma paved the way not only for disaster medicine and emergency relief but also for the treatment of psychiatric trauma, which shares the same origins.[34] Constant exposure to risk and suffering were often presented as two sides of the same damaging context. Diaries and memoirs almost invariably recounted moments of considerable anxiety and sometimes informal support networks, but seldom formal debriefing processes—even for wounded medical personnel and prisoners. Convalescence was often the term used to describe recovery from the exertions of humanitarian work. Most of the suffering was framed in religious tones that made eschatological sense: "We passed safely out of this valley of the shadow of death", reported the surgeon at the hospital in Kars, the site of a decisive but bloody Russian victory during the 1877–1878 Russo-Turkish War.[35]

For much of the nineteenth and twentieth centuries, this religious or spiritual undertaking of dangerous activities, a kind of often humble but heroic economy of risk-taking in the face of increasingly violent events, dominated and existed alongside the accounting and actuarial understanding of risk that the humanitarian enterprise represented. This accommodation of two logics, seemingly contradictory, was facilitated by the rudimentary bureaucratic processes adopted by humanitarian agencies and the autonomy made necessary by distance from headquarters. Retrospective accounts and letters from the field present evidence of both logics in the same documents. It is striking that risk was not quantified and security remained a loose and deflationary concept. In conflict situations, people were at risk, security was relative and whoever was granting safe passage might be unable to do so the next day. All employers could do was to rely on vague assurances from third parties—and hope for the best.

Furthermore, contractual agreements with volunteers were radically at odds with contemporary employment law. Since the close of the nineteenth century, the liability of the employer in civilian society across Europe had been presumed over that of the employee (only the employee's negligence had to be proved as the cause of the accident rather than, as in the past, simply presuming it) but the rule did not apply to volunteers. This loophole remains in practice, even if many voluntary organisations since the 1870s have paid full-time humanitarians a per diem, salary or stipend. In this specific contractual arrangement, which is more of an informal convention than actual law, the volunteer is an associate rather than an employee of a humanitarian agency.

Of course, even then, this was largely a fiction and many employees did not volunteer for risk-taking. The distinction between a hired employee and a paid volunteer remains obscure. For instance, Henry Dunant's Solferino coachman had not bargained on risking his life when he took his passenger, nor were the more menial ambulance employees in Kars expecting their fate to be abandoned to the Russians. The culture of risk-taking and danger-facing was, to some extent, self-mythologising and self-glorifying, more revealing of how humanitarians told their stories than of the realities they faced in the field or the risk they imposed on others.[36]

Some years after the Franco-Prussian War, the German lawyer Carl Lüder produced an emotionless survey that won the Augusta Prize for the best book on humanitarian work. A severe critique of self-congratulatory humanitarian narratives, it echoed scathing military criticisms of the relevance and legitimacy of humanitarians in conflict situations.[37] Combatants rejected the encumbrance of amateur humanitarians while they were winning and found the benefit of their relief work unreliable when they needed it.[38] Yet Lüder had failed to appreciate, as have many military commentators since, how entrenched the legitimacy of the Geneva principles had become in the practices of modern war, even though, or perhaps even because, these had often been ignored during the war itself. Furthermore, narratives on the Franco-Prussian War were intended to establish the precedent for later interventions.

At this early stage of the provision of international humanitarian aid in situations of war, the promoting of a new emblem, the new set of principles drafted in Geneva and new legitimacy rooted in an unprecedented delivery of aid and the emphasis on the voluntary and gratuitous nature of humanitarian work were all part of historical humanitarian narratives. This quest for legitimacy was also founded on the modernity of humanitarian aid, the promises of international law[39] and the enthusiasm inspired by new compassionate attitudes. Yet it became a narrative process early on. By the time the first Nobel Peace Prize was awarded to Henry Dunant in 1901,[40] the mass of these narratives—by then a dense forest of pamphlets, books and plays (such as Wilkie Collins's *The New Magdalen* published in 1873 and set in the Franco-Prussian War)—developed legitimacy, as the expression of civilisation in wartime. These accounts affirmed and asserted the effectiveness of the protective, almost talisman, status of humanitarian aid flags for staff as well as their "beneficiaries", despite overwhelming evidence to the contrary.

The Dialectic of Security and Protection

This broad historical frame for interpreting the foundations of humanitarian notions of risk and security is intended to show how intrinsically bound these are with origin myth and ideals of humanitarianism. First appearing in the conflicts of the late nineteenth century, the evaluation framework of violence was both statistical and sentimental, enshrining protection and its violation. It relied as much on probability calculations as on emotional responses to danger. The reliance on emblems to afford—and not simply represent—protection lived on in a world dominated by increasingly sophisticated attempts to evaluate and monitor risk and avert danger.

Protecting with Numbers

This statistical intent to quantify risk and exposure along with the scale of violence has been central for modern humanitarians. Current efforts to quantify what is war, using the Uppsala index or various other statistical indicators, do not make much sense in "real-time" and lend themselves to retrospective controversies.[41] The attempts to qualify the Vietnam War or Biafra as genocide illustrated how the two modes of evaluation could correlate and how emotional responses could call on statistical evidence in political discourse. The notion of humanitarian intervention, which, as historians such as Davide Rodogno have shown, has its roots in the engagement of Western powers with specific Christian groups in the Ottoman Empire, was still alive at the onset of World War Two.[42] The challenge humanitarian intervention poses to the principle of state sovereignty was known as much then as now. The revival of principles and practices after the end of the Cold War renewed utopian dreams that humanitarian aid might be more than an emblem of good intentions and actually deliver effective protection. Of course, the evidence shows that it failed repeatedly, because humanitarians were unable to protect themselves, let alone others. From the failure to maintain "safe havens" during the Bosnian War to the massacre of (national) humanitarian workers in Rwanda, there is no shortage of examples in the 1990s not only of the demonstrable inefficiency of UN protection but also of humanitarian emblems.

If the ability to protect fell far short of the aspirations that were sometimes assigned to aid, security concerns in the meantime grew in reverse proportion. Within organisations, the assimilation of danger to risk, risk management to security, security to safety, collapsed hitherto specific and separate cultural and linguistic categories. Until the 1990s, risk avoidance was perfectly compatible with the notion of exposure to danger. Orbinski, former international president of MSF, relates in his "ego-narrative" a revealing exchange with MSF worker "Joni" in Somalia in 1992 that echoed some of the trade-offs of 1990s humanitarianism. Surrounded by the sound of machine gun fire, and despite the ambient danger, the humanitarian worker argued that there was no risk: "If we get killed, NGOs will withdraw and there will be no one to pay protection racket or wages. They want us scared and alive. So you should be scared and happy because it means you can work."[43]

Implemented to gauge and assess danger, many of the measures taken since the 1990s have shunned this logic of heroics. The economic trade-off between perpetrators of violence and humanitarian workers remains but cannot be the security approach employers adopt when deploying staff in the field. Insecurity became an inflationary concept, as humanitarian organisations grew and came to realise the full extent of their duties and liabilities as employers. Perhaps necessarily, humanitarians have come to terms with the size of their operations and their bureaucracy has generated human resources policies commensurate with their funding, possibly closing the gap between the fiction of volunteering and their duties as employers. In this workplace as in others, maybe there should be signs stating that "employees have the right to work without threats" and not to be exposed to a "hostile environment". Perceptions engendered from data have progressively taken precedence over those acquired in the field as risk evaluations become the focus of security analyses. This seems a dangerous drift, however, since it is that fiction of volunteering that was the condition required for "charity under fire" to exist in the first place.

The Field "Under Control"

There is an obvious paradox in security evidence garnered in the field when, arguably, security processes are increasingly dominant in defining the field itself. The late Lisa Smirl argued, when considering the impact of machines and humanitarian spaces, and the role of the ubiquitous 4WD and bunker-like compounds in the shaping of humanitarian perceptions of the world, the field as experienced by humanitarian aid workers is constituted of and mediated through various filters and boundaries. These are not only visible but also implicit.[44] What humanitarians call the "field" is often lived in daylight, limited by strict curfews to what amounts to only half a day in equatorial and tropical countries. As the tinted windows in fast cars provide a filtered perception of the world, the design of humanitarian programmes that include risk assessments from the outset filter humanitarian perceptions of the field. Since the advent in the 1990s of cost-effective rapid communications, the increasingly common deployment of reliable satellite phones and even the Internet, the field has become more elastic as it is shared across continents between headquarter-based programme managers and their security apparatus and the staff on the ground. The issues of remote control and the politics of risk management identified by Mark Duffield have grown from this sense that events can indeed be portrayed as accurately from headquarters as from the actual field—no longer a first-hand experience but one of shared data management.[45]

Generating data to encode the experience of staff in the field empowers nobody in particular[46] but raises new notions of risk and danger at headquarters and country capital levels. The vertical transmission of information from the field to head office is then reciprocated through the sometimes real-time transmission of guidelines and security guidance. It is frequently implemented through the issuing of consolidated, often more extensive, rules complying with the inflationary modus operandi of risk assessments.[47]

When distance was part of the humanitarian "adventure" and it could take weeks for orders and guidelines to get through, the field was constituted in a very different manner, largely through a sequence of small negotiations. These ensured some degree of security, primarily with more or less reliable gatekeepers and intermediaries who were subject to individual assessments varying from individual to individual. The same setting could be viewed as safe or unsafe by two successive teams, each with their own evaluation of the risks. In reality, these encounters of a profound human nature continue today and so do their differences. Yet gatekeepers and local security brokers have been downgraded as to their importance to security—to trust too much risks becoming a form of negligence for humanitarian organisations and their personnel alike.

This is not entirely new, of course, as the notion of unreliable and dubious intermediaries benefiting from their roles as go-betweens for the rich incomer and hostile locals dates back to colonial times. Crooks and folk heroes, such as Hampaté Bâ's character Wangrin,[48] have been the focus of many books exploring the role of intermediaries in the colonial setting. Humanitarians directly inherit rules from the colonial and imperial era when they employ staff whose role is to be on-going intermediaries for transient and profoundly ignorant international staff.[49]

Risk-evaluations are all inclusive and potentially destructive of the notion of trust upon which many humanitarian encounters rely. They do not allow broad spaces for negotiation and, through their transposition from one location to another, the filling in of risk assessment forms demands an ever-higher degree of pre-conceived suspicion.

Of course, the dramatic evolution described here is historically contingent. It reflects other forms of power concentration and the tightening of chains of command supported by technological innovation. On one level, it is rooted in the notion that responsibility should always imply control and that control is rooted in management. It also implies that "duty of care", as enshrined in employment legislation, confers overwhelming decisional rights and that, conversely, the individual is neither responsible nor careful. Arguably, this loss of autonomy is not restricted to the humanitarian sector as it is widely prevalent in Western societies. It relies on fictions of control and accountability as heroic as yesteryear's fictions of daredevilry with their assumptions of frictionless mechanisms and fool proof guidance. Humanitarian staff create solidarity in their work in the field through small acts of resistance to the smooth machinery of securitisation, and disobedience frequently becomes a badge of honour. Small transgressions become the stuff of the field as they compensate to some degree for the curtailing of operational and personal space while exposing daily the vacuity of excessive narratives of danger.

In the humanitarian context, extreme securitisation rooted in worst-case-scenario and all-eventuality training comforts critiques of humanitarian aid, more often than not originating from within the aid sector itself, which, since the 1980s, have accused NGOs of being self-serving and self-obsessed. Much of the humanitarian literary output of a critical nature explored by Lisa Smirl and others in books such as *Emergency Sex and Other Desperate Measures* examined in a contradictory manner how NGOs harbour irresponsible and infantilised staff.[50] Within this discourse, humanitarians are over protected and yet, due to their powerlessness and lack of "genuine" expertise, they are exposed to the traumatic consequences of humanitarian aid. This analysis is blatantly circular and indeed narcissistic, but it flows in a continuous stream of self-doubt, relentlessly eroding the legitimacy of humanitarian action.

Far from being an additional marker of increased professionalisation in the field, the progressively dominant approach to security and securitisation in the field amounts to a gradual erosion of the humanitarian worker's sense of agency and responsibility. It also signals the recognition that humanitarian NGOs, similar to large multinational organisations, do not feel sufficiently confident to leave crucial negotiations to their field staff. As a hierarchy carries the burden of responsibility and duty of care, it seems to say, the freedom of distance and autonomy cannot be left to lesser levels in the organisation.

Conclusion

Since 1864, modern humanitarian aid has consistently generated and responded to evaluations of need and risk and this work has been framed by exposure to danger and security concerns. A number of assumptions regarding risk, volunteering and danger have enabled humanitarian workers and NGOs to function in the face of danger. Its emblems embodied this will to work under the protection of the law but they seldom provided protection alone. What enabled humanitarians to work in acutely violent places was a combination of myths about courage, character and adventure, associated with negotiations at the bedrock of very careful risk management. The shift to a "post-heroic" age has profoundly altered how humanitarians relate to each other. The balance between individual agency and collective responsibility, between volunteering for and exposing staff to danger, was always delicate. It tipped toward responsibility and duty of care with the advent of bureaucratic decision processes (rather than the bureaucracies themselves, which have always been a necessary and valuable component of humanitarian aid organisations).

Arguably, bureaucratic decision processes have depended on the ability to translate field concerns into security guidelines, which emerged early on in some organisations and somewhat belatedly in others. The culture specific to each NGO would undoubtedly nuance the broad-brush argument presented here; Michaël Neuman's chapter charters much more precisely the evolution of risk perception and security management within MSF.

In the broad historical perspective, documenting violence affecting humanitarians was framed in the heroic logic of volunteering and possible sacrifice. It invited the ghostly presence of international humanitarian law, but this legal framework provided no more safeguards or guarantees than the adopting of a heroic logic. In a world that has applied the logic of humanitarianism to justify interventions—military and diplomatic—since at least 1860,[51] humanitarians have remained bound to the negotiations that have enabled them to define the duration and nature of their stay or their "terrain", now called "the field". The imagining of a global order based on protection bypassed these concerns to foster a focus on security processes, a gathering of data which did not necessarily feed into any planning but rather into even more gathering of data.[52] This securitisation based on numbers and guidelines prescribes behaviours that have always been part of the landscape of humanitarian aid and which appear to have taken on an existence all of their own.

THEORIES

4

VIOLENCE AGAINST AID WORKERS

THE MEANING OF MEASURING

Fabrice Weissman[1]

Quoting statistics on humanitarian insecurity in 2009, the delegate in charge of security at the International Committee of the Red Cross lamented, "the world is a riskier place to be an aid worker."[2] Not a new observation, there is now quantitative data to support it. For the past fifteen years, researchers and consultants have been busy carrying out studies aimed at "quantifying on an objective basis"[3] violence against humanitarian workers. Relying on a variety of indicators, these analyses conclude on the whole that deliberate attacks against aid workers are increasing dramatically. They recommend improving data collection to gain a better understanding of the phenomenon for scientific, practical and political purposes. The emphasis on statistics gives rise to at least two questions: does the existing data truly indicate an increase in insecurity? How useful is this data?

The Methodological Weakness of Existing Data

Where do the Statistics on Humanitarian Insecurity Come From?

The first study on "deaths among humanitarian workers" appeared in the *British Medical Journal* in July 2000.[4] Conducted by epidemiologists from the Johns

Hopkins Bloomberg School of Public Health (Baltimore) with WHO support, it looked at the deaths reported by thirty-two "humanitarian organisations" during the period 1985 to 1998. Johns Hopkins researchers also participated in two cross-sectional studies assessing the prevalence of non-lethal violence[5] and the risk of violence-related morbidity/mortality in the aid sector.[6]

Accessible online, the Aid Worker Security Database (AWSD)[7] is meant to record every "major incident of violence against aid workers" (i.e. "killings, kidnappings and attacks that result in serious injury") reported by the media and aid operators since 1997. An offshoot of a 2006 study conducted for the Overseas Development Institute (ODI) and the Center on International Cooperation,[8] the AWSD is now kept up-to-date by Humanitarian Outcomes (HO), a consulting firm set up by the authors of the 2006 study. HO releases an annual report on the security of aid workers, the source of data most frequently cited by the media, the United Nations, NGOs and humanitarian security experts.[9] AWSD figures and analyses will be the main subject of this chapter.

With the Insecurity Insight group,[10] a third source of statistics appeared in 2008. The group, comprising two academics (a statistician and a conflict specialist), a medical advisor from the International Committee of the Red Cross (ICRC) and a humanitarian consultant, has developed in partnership with several NGOs its own database, the Security in Numbers Database (SiND).[11] Insecurity Insight also contributes to quantitative studies conducted by the ICRC as part of its Health Care in Danger campaign launched in 2011.[12]

How Accurate are the Indicators?

All of these studies claim to be "evidence-based", but careful reading reveals several methodological weaknesses. The first stems from the indicators selected to translate the abstract concepts of insecurity, danger and violence into quantitative data. While the AWSD and Johns Hopkins look at the number of aid workers killed, injured or kidnapped, the ICRC and Insecurity Insight studies count all security events affecting humanitarian work or healthcare—considered a more pertinent indicator for describing the daily violence hampering humanitarian action. Thus, in addition to attacks against personnel, they record incidents as varied as bombings, thefts of supplies and equipment, arrests of patients, threats or damage to the aid agencies' reputation, water shortages and electricity outages, and administrative obstacles.

With no precise boundaries, the notion of an "incident affecting humanitarian work" is extremely vague and subject to interpretation, and this weakens its value as an accurate and meaningful indicator. The better defined category of "aid workers killed, injured or kidnapped" is not much easier to use, necessitating as it does that one should determine whether the victims were harmed as a result of their work, and whether that work was "humanitarian". There is of course no generally accepted definition of "humanitarian work" among practitioners, researchers, authorities, military personnel or journalists. The first Johns Hopkins mortality study counted UN peacekeeping forces among humanitarian organisations, whereas the AWSD excludes armed forces, human rights workers and people working on "reconstruction projects." Instead, it defines aid workers as national and international employees and commercial subcontractors of "not-for-profit aid agencies [...] that provide material and technical assistance in humanitarian relief contexts." This somewhat tautological definition leaves those tasked with updating the database much room for interpretation. In reality, the "aid worker" category is applied to a wide range of actors who differ in terms of status, functions, practices and, therefore, exposure to danger: representatives of foreign governments and funding bodies; UN officials and employees; representatives of the ICRC and the Federation; national Red Cross and Red Crescent society volunteers; employees of international and local NGOs; members of religious and community solidarity networks; employees of transport and private security companies, etc.

Determining whether attacks are related to the victims' work is also problematic, particularly for national staff (over 90 per cent of workers) who, in addition to their professional activities, are exposed to "ordinary" crime and war-related violence. In practice, the databases and studies record every event affecting an aid sector employee or subcontractor, whatever the circumstances. In Syria, for example, the AWSD records national employees killed when their homes were bombed, in an attack on a market, or when the relief convoy they were escorting was machine-gunned. Similarly, in Afghanistan, it counts international staff killed in an attack on a restaurant, while hiking in the forest, during a domestic burglary or during an attack on the hospital where they were working.

How Reliable are the Techniques Used to Collect the Data?

The imprecision of the indicators is further increased by the bias of the methods used to collect the data. The AWSD and SiND databases, as well as the Johns Hopkins epidemiological studies, count attacks and victims based on their reporting in the administrative records of aid organisations and/or the media. AWSD investigators, for instance, rely on information from "public sources, through systematic media filtering [in particular, Relief Web and US

State Department reports], and provided directly to the project by aid organisations"[13] such as UNDSS, regional security consortiums and MSF.

There is a flaw in this method that is well-known to security specialists: it does not determine whether it is the phenomenon being studied (the violence) that is changing, its reporting (documenting by administrative departments in humanitarian organisations or the media) or some combination of the two.[14] However reliable, media coverage of attacks against aid workers depends on several factors: the number of journalists in the country concerned and the extent of their interest in humanitarian security issues; the nationality of the victims; the transparency of the aid organisations; the feasibility of investigation, etc. Similarly, the systems used by humanitarian organisations to collect security data have improved considerably over the past twenty years, gradually leading to an increase in the type and number of attacks reported. Even so, reporting and transmission of information is still highly dependent on the proactivity of managers, how much resistance they encounter in their organisation, and how much importance their personnel attach to security issues. This can vary greatly over both time and space; while some volunteers are reluctant to collect data on violent incidents,[15] others are inclined to report any type of event likely to affect their security.[16] Therefore, it is difficult to distinguish between changes in violence and changes in the way it is reported, both administratively and in the media. This uncertainty is particularly pronounced for events whose definition is open to interpretation (such as attacks resulting in "serious injuries")[17] and incidents involving national staff (the reporting of which is even more erratic).

Studies attempting to calculate attack and victim rates (number of violent events and victims, respectively, per 100,000 workers per year) face a further obstacle: the lack of a reliable denominator. Rare is the organisation able to provide accurate figures on its workforce by country and by year, and so, for example, the AWSD is forced to put forward a rough estimate of the number of humanitarian workers based on standard budget to national and international staff ratios.[18] Moreover, aside from the AWSD database, all of the studies use samples for which there is no explicit sampling method, other than the ability of the organisations consulted to supply data for the study. Yet they generalise their results to the entire aid sector.

Most of the authors acknowledge that their datasets are neither "complete" nor "fully representative,"[19] that there are "incomplete or missing records"[20] and that the data is "to a degree, inaccurate",[21] particularly with respect to national staff. But they have no doubts about the solidity of the conclusions they draw from them; the Johns Hopkins researchers, for example, "believe the findings to be representative"[22] and Humanitarian Outcomes claims that the "AWSD remains the sole comprehensive global source of this data, providing the evidence base for analysis of the changing security environment."[23]

The Debatable Interpretation of Trends

The Hidden Stability of Victim Rates

All the studies and quantitative analyses conclude, like Insecurity Insight, that there are "rising burdens of insecurity for aid workers."[24] The Johns Hopkins group claims, "Our findings confirm the belief that deaths among humanitarian workers have increased (…) Humans with weapons rather than motor vehicles pose the greatest threat."[25] Similarly, the ODI/HO studies stress the steady decline in security conditions since at least 1997. "Both the numbers of attacks on humanitarian aid operations and the victims they claimed reached their highest point since data has been systematically collected,"[26] declared Humanitarian Outcomes in its 2014 annual report.

The details in these studies, however, hint at a more nuanced situation. Published in 2000, the first Johns Hopkins mortality study described a bell curve: a sharp increase in deaths (all causes combined) from 1985 to 1994—the year of the genocide in Rwanda—followed by a decline from 1995 to 1998. It added that these changes went hand-in-hand with the increase in humanitarian agencies and workers in the field. But, with no data on the number of people deployed, it was unable to draw any conclusions about the change in risk.

This was precisely the limitation that the ODI/HO studies sought to overcome. Estimating the transformation in the humanitarian workforce, they calculated the variation in the attack rates (number of security events per 100,000 workers per year) and victim rates (number of people killed, injured or kidnapped per 100,000 workers per year). Unlike the absolute data, the relative data received little public attention. The AWSD website only provides graphs illustrating the trebling of the attack rate from 1997 to 2012[27] (cf. figure 1) while victim rates are only mentioned in three reports—in 2006,[28] 2009[29] and 2013.[30]

Yet, whereas the annual number of victims has quadrupled in absolute terms over the past fifteen years (from seventy-eight for the 1997–2001 period to 376 in 2012–2013, cf. table 1), in relative terms it has remained remarkably stable; from 1997 to 2012, the number of workers killed, injured or kidnapped per 100,000 per year fluctuated between forty and sixty (cf. figure 2).[31] In other words, according to AWSD's own data, the number of victims has increased in proportion to the number of aid workers. In this sense, humanitarian action is no more dangerous than it was in the past. The risk of violent death may even be dropping, if we believe the decline in the percentage of deaths among victims (from 49 per cent in 1997–2001 to 30 per cent in 2012–2013, according to the author's calculations using the AWSD database). Surprisingly, the 2013 report draws the opposite conclusion, stating in its summary that the "number of victims relative to the estimated total number of aid workers (...) continued to rise."[32]

Figure 1: Number of attacks per 10,000 aid workers and per year (1997–2012, AWSD 2013)[33]

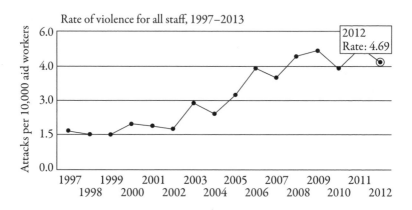

Figure 2: Number of aid workers killed, seriously injured or kidnapped per 100,000 aid workers per year (1997–2012, AWSD)

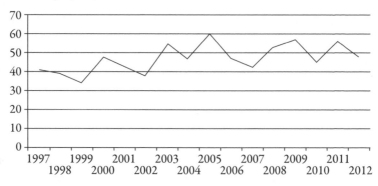

Sources: AWSD 2009[34] (1997–2005) and AWSD 2013[35] (2006–2012).

Table 1: Number of victims among humanitarian personnel, yearly average (sources: AWSD, author's calculations)

	1997–2001		2002–2006		2007–2011		2012–2013	
Killed	38	49%	64	42%	97	36%	113	30%
Kidnapped	24	31%	29	19%	78	29%	117	31%
Injured	16	20%	60	39%	96	36%	147	39%
Total	78	100%	153	100%	271	100%	376	100%

No Global Trend

The overall stability of the rates—like the overall increase in the absolute number of victims—masks wide disparities between different countries and different years. More than half of the deaths considered by Johns Hopkins from 1985 to 1998 occurred in the African Great Lakes region and the Horn of Africa. And three-quarters of the victims listed by the AWSD since 1997 have been in only six or seven countries.[36]

Even among the highest-risk countries, the homicide rate for humanitarian workers varies widely. According to the 2012 AWSD report,[37] for the period 2006–2011, it ranged from 3/100,000/year in the Democratic Republic of Congo (the same order of magnitude as the homicide rate in the United States) to 9/100,000/year in the two Sudans, Afghanistan and Pakistan, to 17/100,000/year in Central African Republic, to 37/100,000/year in Sri Lanka, and to 58/100,000/year in Somalia.

It is difficult to establish whether these rates reveal that humanitarian workers are more exposed than other people. This would require comparing them to the homicide rate within the population as a whole or to other categories such as journalists, small traders, truckers, etc. It should be emphasised, however, that homicide rates for humanitarian workers are lower than that of fatal accidents among the most dangerous civilian professions in the United States, namely logging workers (91 deaths per 100,000 workers per year), fishermen (75/100,000/year) and aircraft pilots and flight engineers (50/100,000/year).[38]

Contradictory Interpretation of the Observed Variations

ODI/HO interprets the rarity of attacks in the majority of settings as proof of "improved security management throughout the humanitarian community."[39] That is, the professionalism of aid actors has helped protect relief workers, including in situations "marked by high crime or societal disruption". They explain the abnormally high death rate in the six or seven highest-risk countries by the extremism and unbridled violence of the belligerents, which no amount of protection can counter. In other words, while improved security conditions can be credited to aid actors, worsening security can be blamed on the assailants.

Insecurity Insight, on the other hand, attributes increased insecurity to "greater humanitarian presence in dangerous contexts," particularly in "areas of active fighting and [in] urban areas, where crime is a bigger issue." Subject to pressure by the media and funders, they say, humanitarian actors show "higher risk tolerance", working in environments from which they would, in the past, have withdrawn.[40]

The data exploited in these studies cannot be used to determine which of these interpretations is correct, even in a given country or situation. A qualitative approach is needed to distinguish between changes that are due to the context and those due to the practices of aid agencies. In this case, neither ODI/HO nor Insecurity Insight offer empirical evidence to justify their preferred interpretations. These appear to mirror their preconceptions regarding insecurity, with Insecurity Insight lamenting an aid system resigned to losing personnel and HO bemoaning a world that has become increasingly violent toward humanitarian workers.

The Question of Targeting

Finally, the ODI/HO studies aimed "to measure to what extent aid workers were targeted specifically for reasons related to their mission."[41] To achieve this, they calculated the respective proportions of "incidental" violence unrelated to the fact that the victims were aid workers ("wrong time, wrong place"), and "political" and "economic" violence, targeting aid workers as such ("because they were aid workers").

They concluded that the majority of attacks listed since 1997 were political rather than incidental. More precisely, aid workers were said to be targeted because they are "perceived to be aligned or equated with another party (the US, the West, the UN)". As, for example, HO explained in 2011, "[A]ntipathy toward an international humanitarian presence perceived as Western-aligned, continue[s] to drive overall trends in attack numbers."[42] Sri Lanka and the Palestinian Occupied Territories were, however, considered exceptions to the rule. The high humanitarian worker death rate from 2006 to 2011 was felt to be incidental—"collateral damage" caused by intense fighting.

The authors of the 2006 initial study clarify that they were, however, unable to make "a reasonable judgment as to motivations"[43] of the attackers in three out of five cases. In fact, it is often difficult to identify the perpetrators and their sponsors with any certainty, and even less to know their intentions and primary targets. Were they targeting the individual in a private capacity, the various institutions that the victim represented—employer, family, government, nation, patron, neighbourhood, political party, social class, religious or ethnic community—or an unrelated third party?

In practice, ODI/HO reports provide no quantitative (or qualitative) data demonstrating that humanitarian actors are targeted primarily because they represent an aid sector equated with the West, rather than because of a perception that they are bad bosses, malevolent doctors, economic competitors or allies of the opposition. The hypothesis attributing violence against humanitarian workers to their real or assumed lack of neutrality is, on the contrary, belied by ODI/HO's own data, with the 2006 report showing no correlation between the number of violent events and the presence of Western troops or UN integrated missions,[44] and the 2013 report describing an increase in the number of attacks in Afghanistan—after the withdrawal of NATO troops.[45]

In fact, the hypothesis that the violence is associated with the "undeniably Western nature and orientation of much of the international aid community"[46] obscures the political transactions upon which the security of humanitarian actors depends. As we have shown elsewhere,[47] relief operation deployment depends not on abstract principles such as neutrality, impartiality and independence, but on negotiating an acceptable compromise with the various forces present, at the intersection of the different parties' interests and constraints. To put it bluntly, the protection of aid actors depends on their ability to find an acceptable way—if there is one—to be more useful alive than dead to those committing the violence. And there is no evidence to suggest that their "Western nature" is an insurmountable obstacle to this; indeed, the impressive ICRC and MSF deployment in Afghanistan—ten years after being among the Taliban's primary designated targets—demonstrates quite the opposite.

The Production of Ignorance

Is Increasing Humanitarian Insecurity a "Myth"?

In summary, quantitative studies on humanitarian insecurity are based on unreliable indicators whose ambiguous meaning is systematically interpreted in such a way that confirms the preconception that danger is escalating. Does this mean that increasing humanitarian insecurity is a "myth", as, for example, criminologist Arnaud Dandoy and political scientist Marc-Antoine Pérouse de Montclos[48] claim?

As these two authors rightly point out, the history of humanitarian action has been punctuated by deliberate attacks against aid workers, from the 1870 Franco-Prussian War through both World Wars, the wars of independence and the Cold War to the extreme crises of the 1990s.[49] As for the past fifteen years, some findings might withstand critical examination of the existing data: while there has been an increase in the absolute number of humanitarian workers killed, injured or kidnapped, this increase appears to be proportional to the growing number of humanitarian personnel. Moreover, the majority of incidents are concentrated in a small number of countries. Serious attacks against aid workers are therefore neither new, nor widespread, nor growing in relative terms.

This does not mean, however, that the rise in insecurity is a myth or that the concerns expressed by aid actors are irrational. The evolution in attacks against humanitarian workers indistinctively reflects developments in the political and military context and in the security practices of aid organisations. In this sense, the relative stability in the victim rate since 1997 may conceal a worsening security environment compensated by better protection measures and/or the withdrawal of aid organisations from the most dangerous areas.[50] In any event, interpreting trends requires using other sources—qualitative, in particular—to evaluate how dangers and security practices are changing, context by context.

"Not everything that counts can be counted" (Albert Einstein)[51]

And yet aid actors and specialists are less concerned with rounding out quantitative studies with historical or sociological approaches than with producing better and more complete, accurate and reliable figures. This predilection for numbers—despite their weak descriptive or analytical power—has mainly to do with the agenda of those doing the quantifying. "What gets counted gets done!" says, for example, an author of an ICRC study, whose stated goal was to produce "reliable data" to influence "the policies of all stakeholders [...] in favour of greater security of effective and impartial health care in armed conflict."[52] Hence the primary goal of producing numbers is not to understand the mechanisms behind the attacks, but to denounce their existence (without having to describe them in detail). Reinforcing edifying narratives, the data are used to construct a new, intolerable moral around the violence done to humanitarian workers, and more particularly healthcare workers.

Indeed, the very notion of attacks against humanitarian workers suggests that they are targeted because of their status by attackers who reject the values of humanism and solidarity these workers claim to represent; or, that they are hurt in spite of their status, which is supposed to protect them by virtue of their "exceptional" social and moral value.[53] In either case, aid actors are seen as the heroic victims of evil incarnate or of cynical usurpers who have weakened the protective powers of their logos. The codes and formalism of science are used to bolster this view by treating weak, equivocal insecurity data as facts that "cannot reasonably be questioned."[54]

The legitimacy and effectiveness of such an activist strategy are questionable. As Patrice Bourdelais and Didier Fassin remind us, the construction of one intolerable is inseparable from tolerance for another intolerable.[55] In this case, defending humanitarians in danger has replaced defending populations in danger—the focus of public opinion campaigns by aid actors in the 1990s. It is not evident that humanitarians, as a group, should be more sacrosanct than journalists, small traders, farmers, drivers, mechanics, or non-combatants in general. Also questionable is the political efficacy of campaigns that refuse to name the perpetrators of serious violence—or even the countries where it occurs in the case of the ICRC—in order "to avoid giving rise to political controversy."[56]

However, the biggest problem with abusing quantitative data for activist purposes is that it produces ignorance. Beyond the uncertainty surrounding the reliability and meaning of the statistics, global figures convey the misleading notion that the violence is a global phenomenon obeying general laws.[57] In practice, searching for common causes results in the dominant prejudices in the aid world—attributing insecurity to the lack of real or assumed neutrality as well as to anti-Western sentiment—being presented as scientific fact. They also result in relatively infrequent, heterogeneous events in a wide range of volatile settings being lumped together into a single aggregate in the hopes of detecting statistically significant trends, probabilities and risk factors. Sometimes comparing violence to a disease, such global quantitative approaches nourish the illusion that security dilemmas can be clarified, or even solved, by mathematically calculating incidence rates and risk–benefit ratios.

In so doing, quantitative studies divert the attention of practitioners and specialists away from the real challenge, which is to analyse each major secu-

rity event, to place it in the local historical context and that of the relief operation, to discuss the practices that contributed to its occurrence (or mitigation)
and whether the risks were worth taking. In order to understand and prevent
violence, we must tackle the sensitive questions hidden by the quantification
exercise—in particular, who is perpetrating the violence, and which mistakes,
if any, are aid actors making? This is not to say, of course, that we should
abandon all efforts to quantify. For a particular organisation or situation,
keeping count of violent acts that result in human and material damage is
necessary, if only to facilitate their qualitative analysis. While it is important
to record incidents scrupulously, it is even more urgent to use substantiated
accounts in order to understand how and why they happened.

SECURITY INCIDENT NARRATIVES BURIED IN NUMBERS: THE MSF EXAMPLE

Fabrice Weissman[58]

Since 1971, thirteen international staff members have been killed while on assignment with MSF. Five volunteers were assassinated in Somalia (1997, 2008 and 2011),[59] four in Afghanistan (1990 and 2004),[60] two in Sudan (1989),[61] one in Angola (1992)[62] and one in Central African Republic (2007).[63] However, there has been no reliable data on the number of national employees who have been killed while on mission or on the number of staff (national or international) seriously injured or kidnapped since the founding of MSF.

In 2009, in response to this lack of information and confirming the recommendations provided by security specialists,[64] MSF introduced a system to collect data on safety and security incidents known as SINDY.[65] Developed by MSF-Belgium, all MSF operational sections progressively adopted (and adapted) SINDY via their respective security advisors.

Directly updated by the teams in the field, the database is restricted to the organisation's managers, who have access rights which vary according to their level of responsibility.[66] SINDY combines three functions: centralised archiving for incident reports,[67] quantitative data collection[68] and an alert system.[69] Each MSF operational section has its own database to which it alone has access, although this does not prevent the occasional sharing of incident or summary reports.

SINDY's scope of application varies from one section to another. Whether safety incidents (road accidents, blood exposure, electrical accidents, etc.) are recorded or not, SINDY's various databases are based on disparate case definitions. For instance, MSF-France restricts encoding to moderate and severe security incidents with consequences on property or people[70] whereas MSF-Belgium asks users to log any security and safety incident presenting a high, medium or low risk to property, people or operations.[71] MSF-Spain has extended the database to events affecting "the acceptance and/or neutrality of MSF."[72]

To date, SINDY has been primarily used by security advisors to produce annual year-end quantitative reports on security management; a summary for the year 2014 is provided below for the three main operational centres (Belgium, France, Holland). All the reports highlight that theft and threats make up the majority of incidents reported, while warning against making hasty interpretations of this data given the reporting bias observed in the field. MSF-Belgium underlines that the sharp fall in the number of incidents recorded in 2014 (cf. Table 2) "is not linked with a real decrease of incidents in the field but with the fact of the decrease of the reporting itself."[73] Conversely, the Dutch section attributes the increased number of incidents seen in 2014 to its improved reporting system but also to the fact that "respect for independent humanitarian action is diminishing."[74]

MSF-Holland and MSF-France reports are alone in including a succinct description of the circumstances and consequences of the most serious events recorded in 2014, such as the unresolved abduction of four Congolese employees in the Democratic Republic of Congo in 2013, the murder of nineteen people (including one patient and three national staff members) at two hospitals managed by MSF in Central African Republic, the detention since 2012 of a national staff member in Burma and the looting and destruction of three hospitals in South Sudan. Deprived of the benefit of a more detailed description, MSF-Belgium's report lauds the fact that, in 2014, the organisation "did not face a strong increase in severe incidents [showing] the capacity of the organisation to adapt and work in very sensitive contexts."[75] The report makes no mention of the kidnap that same year in Syria of the five expatriates working for the Belgium section who were freed between three and five months later after being held in particularly harsh conditions.

The quantitative approach to insecurity adopted by MSF and the way it is used reveal the same failings generally observed in other similar databases, such as the Aid Worker Security Database.[76] Relying on ambiguous definitions without any consistency between sections, MSF's data is diminished by significant reporting bias[77]—all the more because it concerns a small number of very disparate incidents, which results in data devoid of any real statistical significance. And lastly, shrinking the description of each event to make it fit into a generic nomenclature ("theft", "threat", "kidnapping", etc.), the quantitative description of incidents impoverishes their understanding and masks each one's particular significance. By way of example, SINDY aggregates into the same category "threats" made by ISIS militants against MSF volunteers suspected of spying, "threats" made to a field coordinator by a representative of striking staff in CAR and "threats" issued against a doctor by the parents of a patient admitted to the Khamer hospital in Yemen. All threats but, needless to say, all completely different, as much in the dangers they pose as in how they should be responded to. Similarly, a quantitative approach to "severe security incidents" allows some MSF security focal points to congratulate themselves on a numerical stability that conceals the unprecedented severity of kidnappings that occurred in 2014.

Just as MSF is investing in building databases on security incidents—in line with the rest of the humanitarian aid sector—the usefulness of such data is being challenged by sectors as sensitive as nuclear energy and air traffic safety.[78] For instance, Eurocontrol (the European Organisation for the Safety of Air Navigation) no longer evaluates the safety of air traffic control operations on the basis of incident data, preferring instead qualitative operational and performance indicators.[79] It notably encourages dialogue between different air traffic control authorities to share information and experience about events occurring on a daily basis, with particular emphasis on particular critical incidents, the importance and severity of which go unnoticed in databases.

In reality, the main advantage of SINDY is to provide a technical solution for systematic and central archiving of incident and accident reports involving national and international personnel. It has yet to serve a useful purpose, i.e. to calculate simple and clear indicators, such as the number of fatal accidents or the number of accidents resulting in sick leave (inexplicably absent from the summary tables currently proposed by SINDY)[80] and to examine and discuss the most serious events based on rigorous qualitative analyses. In this respect, what is lacking at MSF and other humanitarian organisations is not so much a statistics bureau but rather an entity similar to France's civil aviation Bureau d'enquête et d'analyse (BEA, Bureau of Investigation and Analysis), whose mission is:

"To conduct neutral investigation, whose sole purpose is to collect and analyse relevant information, to determine the circumstances and the likely or possible causes of the accident or incident, and, if relevant, to produce safety recommendations to prevent future accident and incident from happening."[81]

Table 2: Security incidents recorded in the SINDY database by MSF-Holland, MSF-Belgium and MSF-France (2010–2014)

	2010	2011	2012	2013	2014
Severe					
MSF-H	–	–	9	10	9
MSF-B	39	52	19	16	22
MSF-F	–	–	–	14	14
Non Severe					
MSF-H	–	–	70	136	195
MSF-B	275	332	303	226	146
MSF-F				59	58
Total					
MSF-H	–	–	79	146	204
MSF-B	314	384	322	242	168
MSF-F	–	–	–	73	72

5

HUMANITARIAN SECURITY MANUALS

NEUTRALISING THE HUMAN FACTOR
IN HUMANITARIAN ACTION

Monique J. Beerli and *Fabrice Weissman*

As described in previous chapters, security-oriented transformations implemented in the past twenty years have left their mark on humanitarian practice. Against this backdrop, the role of "humanitarian security" manuals in formalising security policies and procedures within the humanitarian sector has been significant.

First appearing in 1993 as a series of short pamphlets, in 1999 the ICRC published *Staying Alive*, which included a set of guidelines on how to behave and what to be aware of in a conflict zone, detailed descriptions of weapons used in conflict, and guidance about how to minimise physical harm when under attack.[1] In 1995, Save the Children UK released a guide entitled *Safety First*,[2] the first of its kind by an international NGO to be entirely devoted to security. *Safety First* addressed topics such as the use of humanitarian principles in protection strategies while providing an introduction to security management practices and an overview of practical protection measures.[3]

Subsequent to the Great Lakes crisis, the first security training modules were developed in 1996 as part of a collaborative effort between the United

States Agency for International Development/Office of U.S. Foreign Disaster Assistance (USAID/OFDA) and InterAction. This initiative laid the foundation for what in 2000 became Good Practice Review Number Eight (GPR 8), edited by Koenraad Van Brabant on behalf of the Humanitarian Policy Network at the Overseas Development Institute (ODI, London). Entitled *Operational Security Management in Violent Environments*,[4] the GPR 8 was designed "as a practical reference tool [for] field-level aid agency managers [offering] a systematic step-by-step approach to security management starting from context analysis and threat and risk assessment, to security strategy choice and security planning."

Coordinated by consultants from Humanitarian Outcomes, in 2010 a larger group of experts revised and republished the GPR 8.[5] The revision process called on some thirty contributors and reviewers, with representatives from twenty NGOs (including MSF), three United Nations agencies (UNICEF, UNWFP, UNDSS), three institutional donors (USAID, ECHO, DfID) and seven private companies with connections to security (insurance, corporate security, telecommunications, etc.). Considered a "seminal document in humanitarian operational security management"[6] and often referred to as the "bible" of humanitarian security, the GPR 8 has, since its release in 2000, influenced the burgeoning array of security manuals published by relief organisations themselves, donors and professional networks of security experts.

Drawing primarily on the 2000 and 2010 editions of the GPR 8, this chapter provides a general description of the content and the policy recommendations enshrined in security manuals in order to address the following issues. According to these guidelines, why does security need to be professionalised and institutionalised? What is security and how are humanitarians to be protected? What are the preferred solutions to the challenges they confront in the field? The chapter then highlights some of the underlying assumptions and values conveyed in such technical manuals.

Justifying the Call for Security Professionals

Most specialised manuals put forward three arguments to justify the introduction of security expertise into the humanitarian sector. First, replaying highly mediatised events and citing selective statistical data,[7] many manuals argue that "the number of incidents affecting aid agencies has risen significantly" and the "overall respect for aid agencies and therefore for the 'immunity' of its staff has significantly decreased in recent years."[8] As reiterated in the most recent Save the Children (SCF) security guidelines, "[t]he tragic deaths of our aid worker colleagues in recent years highlight the unprecedented levels of hostility and violence to which we are increasingly exposed in the course of our work."[9]

Alongside discourses on the new era of global humanitarian insecurity and the unparalleled complexity of contemporary crises, present-day manuals also call on legal and ethical arguments. "Ultimately, security management in high-risk areas is both a moral and a legal obligation", argues the revised edition of the GPR 8.[10] In the 1990s, legal frameworks were more commonly evoked to stress the responsibility of host countries, their obligations under international humanitarian law and those of other legal entities granting protection and immunity to international civil servants and humanitarian workers.[11] However, the law is currently used as a means to pressure organisations into instituting and applying security experts' recommendations:

> The legal requirement of duty of care of the employer is becoming increasingly impor-
> tant. Many countries have labour laws that impose obligations on employers to ensure
> safety in the workplace. Although such obligations have rarely been considered in the
> context of international aid work, aid organisations are open to growing legal chal-
> lenges if they fail to properly inform staff about the risks associated with a particular
> assignment, or fail to take all necessary measures to reduce those risks.[12]

Lastly, most security manuals argue that security management cannot be allocated to "managers who lack the requisite skill or competence."[13] "Security management, like gender and the environment, can be regarded as a specialist area. It definitely needs expertise."[14] Aid organisations need to "incorporate the externally developed expertise into in-house knowledge."[15] It would be dangerous to rely on managers whose security competence is grounded solely on longstanding operational experience, as "field experience from a world in which there were fewer threats, greater respect for aid organisations and a habit of risk taking may actually be a liability rather than an asset when it comes to security management."[16]

The author of the first edition of the GPR 8 complained in 2001 that, despite these compelling arguments, some humanitarian organisations were still reluctant to professionalise security management in accordance with the recommendations provided in good practice manuals. Among other reasons, he mainly attributed resistance and hesitation to the conservatism, blindness, incompetence, cynicism, arrogance and mental instability of senior and mid-level humanitarian managers. Their attitudes were characterised as follows:

- The dinosaur reflex: "We can continue doing what we did in the past".
- The ostrich reflex: head in the sand and hope the problem will go away.

- The armchair mentality: non-appreciation of the reality because too far removed from it.
- The accountant reflex: "How are we going to fund this?" "Not if it costs a lot".
- The ignorance or false-knowledge syndrome. (...)
- A discriminatory attitude: "International staff are capital assets, national staff are expendables."
- The career-first mentality: keep quiet about training needs, management weaknesses and even incidents if they might negatively affect chances of promotion.
- The adrenaline-addict syndrome: risk-taking gives a thrill.
- The A-type personality: action-oriented, highly driven, hard to restrain.
- Solidarity under threat: "Stay with endangered populations even if you can't do much to protect them."[17]

Nonetheless, ten years later, the authors of the revised edition of the GPR 8 asserted that the humanitarian sector was slowly succumbing to the claims and policy initiatives of security experts and manuals, "giving rise to a growing professionalism and sophistication in humanitarian security practices and interagency coordination."[18]

Overcoming Danger: Calculability, Planning and Self-Discipline

Few manuals offer a precise definition of what they mean by "security" and "good security management". Seemingly the first attempt to define these terms, the GPR 8 identifies "security" as "freedom from risk or harm resulting from violence or other intentional acts."[19] The scope of potentially harmful situations that have to be taken into consideration differs between the two editions of the GPR 8. While the first edition limits the reach of security management to the "protection of aid personnel and aid agency assets from violence",[20] the revised edition extends protection to the aid agencies' "programmes and reputation."[21] As in the corporate sector, security management in the aid world appears now to encompass the protection of an agency's personnel, property and activities as well as the defence of its image.

The GPR 8 and other such manuals remain ambiguous regarding the desired end state that "good operational security management" is meant to achieve. More or less explicitly recognising that "freedom from risk" is an unattainable objective in war zones, there is a tendency to identify good security management with an absence of "unjustified risks", as illustrated in the introduction to the GPR 8 (2010):

> good operational security management means asking whether the risk is justified in light of the potential benefit of the project or programme, and whether everything possible has been done to reduce the risk and the potential impact of an incident.[22]

The absence of unjustified risk is equated with the implementation of the recommendations set out in the manuals—except, explains (in a kind of disclaimer) the introduction to the GPR 8, when the "circumstances" and one's "situational judgment" prescribe "do[ing] something very different from or even contrary to" the advised course of action.[23]

From Empowering Staff to Managing (In)security

Emerging in the mid-1990s, the first generation of security manuals were primarily aimed at producing a single-source document outlining "need-to-know" information for individuals as they got "used to operating in warzones."[24] For example, the ICRC's security pamphlets, its *Staying Alive* guidelines and Save the Children UK's *Safety First* primarily embraced an 'awareness approach', distinguished by the central claim that "[s]ecurity starts with the individual." *Safety First* was intended as a "reference source to remind [NGO employees] of what to look out for and the questions [they] should be asking [themselves]."[25] This style of manual mainly included "tips" to help field personnel confront the hazards of war zones (how to use radio and satellite communications, how to protect vehicles, cope with the threats posed by landmines, respond in the event of an attack, etc.). In explaining how to use the manual, the author of *Staying Alive* even insists on the need to "combine the contents of this book with your own *common sense and judgment*."[26]

This first generation of manuals included a loose notion of what "successful" risk management required from organisations.[27] Suggestions included hiring experienced staff, providing support services for employees, ensuring equipment was in good working order and giving clear guidelines for staff actions, but did not expand upon these points. A more in-depth and exhaustive approach to security management emerged with the publication of the GPR 8 in 2000. Arguing that "organisational failure cannot be a disproportionately contributing factor to injury or death", this good practice guide explicitly claims that "what is missing is a 'management approach' to security—something that this GPR attempts to offer."[28]

Assessing the Risks

The GPR 8 security management framework adopts a general structure mirroring that of the project management cycle: "Assess, plan, implement (and adjust if needed), review and reassess."[29] In order to assess the risks, the GPR 8

sets out a series of steps, starting with a programme analysis ("the identifica-
tion of 'who you are' and 'what you do'")[30] and a situational analysis (a general
understanding of the history and current dynamics of the conflict, society and
culture, crime, infrastructure and climate).[31] Organisations are then expected
to proceed with a detailed contextual analysis (i.e. an analysis of the actors,
political and military developments, political economy of armed groups and
mapping of violence)[32] and to follow up with a threat assessment.

The latter is defined as "the attempt to examine more systematically the
nature, origin, frequency, and geographical concentration of threats."[33] Threats
to be considered include crime (car-jacking, road banditry, street robberies/
muggings, armed raids/robberies, kidnapping), terror attacks (IEDs, car/
truck bombs, suicide bombers in vehicles, bombings and gun attacks in public
places, grenade attacks on compounds, hostage-taking) and combat/military
activity (shelling, infantry crossfire, landmines).[34]

In order to better understand the context and its threats, and to "predict the
kind of incidents that may be likely in the future,"[35] the revised edition of the
GPR 8 recommends compiling incident databases:

> A reliable overview of reportable incidents around the world, worked through a
> database, allows for greater security analysis at the country, regional and global
> levels. (...) [Such a system] can reveal geographical concentrations of incidents,
> provide insight into the types of incidents taking place and show whether the over-
> all number of incidents is increasing or decreasing.[36]

Based on these analyses, organisations may be expected to produce a risk
assessment culminating in a risk matrix plotting and ranking "threats and
vulnerabilities" according to their "probability and impact."[37] This process
must be conducted "in a structured and disciplined manner" in order to
supress the inherent subjectivity of human nature that "can create a distorted
picture reflecting our unconscious bias."[38]

Elaborating the Strategy

After the risk assessment comes the security strategy. Conceptualised for the
first time in the GPR 8, three ideal types of strategy are proposed, each with
their own "overarching philosophy, application of approaches and use of
resources that frame organisational security management": acceptance, protection, deterrence.[39]

The acceptance strategy is understood as a means to remove or negate
threats by "building relationships with local communities and relevant stake-

holders in the operational area, and obtaining their acceptance and consent for the organisation's presence and its work."[40] Managing perception (and more particularly challenging the perception of aid agencies as "instruments of the Western foreign policies and Western values")[41] is described as a key component of a successful acceptance strategy. As such, it implies "maintain[ing] internal and external consistency in communication",[42] at the local and global level. This is especially important in a globalised world where an increasing number of people have access via the Internet and social media to information about an agency and public statements made on its behalf. The revised edition of the GPR 8 insists that:

> the website, a spokesperson at headquarters and a staff member talking to local media on the ground all say the same thing. All staff, from senior managers to guards and drivers, need to be able to understand and communicate the goals and principles of the organisation. (...) One way to ensure that staff are able to communicate these messages is to develop a simple Question and Answer sheet. (...) If possible, control the final version that goes into the public domain: for example, the content of a written press release is easier to keep under control than a press conference that allows questioning, or a live interview. Beware also of "leaked" statements[43]

In addition, agencies should avoid "public criticism" since "critical public statements are seldom received with gratitude."[44]

> The pursuit and preservation of acceptance may require that agencies stay silent about humanitarian or human rights abuses. Speaking out may create security risks on the ground, or may lead to the agency's expulsion.[45]

More generally, the GPR 8 describes encounters with journalists as a potential source of danger:

> A poorly worded, inaccurate or inflammatory statement can put staff in direct danger and may even result in expulsion from a country. (...)In some situations, the role of international agencies may be so contentious that drawing further attention to it by working with the media would be counter-productive. In this case, develop a good defensive strategy, either refusing to comment, limiting remarks to basic factual information or clarifying misinformation by issuing short reactive statements.[46]

While considering acceptance as "the most appealing security strategy" for humanitarian organisations, the GPR 8 encourages agencies to combine it with "protection and deterrence approaches."[47] A protection strategy "tries to reduce vulnerability in two ways, either by hardening the target or by increasing or reducing its visibility."[48] As for the deterrence approach, it "attempts to deter a threat by posing a counter-threat: essentially discouraging would-be attackers by instilling fear of the consequence they may face."[49] In its most extreme form, it implies the use of armed force. Other forms of deterrence are equally considered, such as the use of legal and diplomatic leverage, the suspension of operations or withdrawal as well as support and protection from "local strongmen."[50] Interestingly, the GPR 8 does not consider the use of public pressure or speaking out as possible deterrents, therefore reducing communication and journalists to potential sources of danger rather than protection.

Standardising Procedures and Behaviours

Lastly, a security strategy is implemented, primarily through the application and enforcement of standard operation procedures (SOPs): "Formally established procedures for carrying out particular operations or dealing with particular situations, specifically regarding how to prevent an incident happening, survive an incident or follow up on an incident as part of the agency's crisis management planning."[51] SOPs are generic procedures, ranging from what to do in the routine day-to-day to how to manage an evacuation, report a critical incident and deal with specific threats.

The GPR 8 insists that any security strategy will be undermined if the staff does not have the "behavioural self-discipline"[52] to comply with the SOPs and other regulatory rules, such as codes of conducts (including codes of sexual conduct). "Irresponsible staff (...) being dismissive about security procedures or overconfident that they can handle any security situation because they have done so for many years" are categorised as a threat as much to themselves as to their colleagues. In order to tame or subdue such behaviours, "security procedures may have to be mandatory, and breaches made a disciplinary offence."[53]

In the same vein, staff displaying symptoms of "negative stress", such as "substance abuse, notably caffeine, alcohol, cigarettes and perhaps drugs, a series of short and casual romantic relationships or unprotected sex",[54] may be unable or unwilling to comply with SOPs and codes of conduct. While it is up to individual staff members to manage their own stress, it is the manager's responsibility to remove staff whose "negative stress" represents a threat both to themselves and to others.

The Implicit Ideology of Security Manuals

Although presented as neutral tools, technical manuals such as the GPR 8 and other security reference books peddle a succession of representations and beliefs. As suggested by Giovalucchi and Olivier de Sardan when discussing "logical frameworks" used by development agencies for the conception and planning of projects, "any public policy instrument carries more or less explicit meanings in terms of political vision and cognitive models. In other words, it conveys a certain ideological and epistemological configuration engrained in its technical structure."[55]

Valorising the Institution

First, the new generation of security manuals conveys an extended notion of security that identifies the institution itself as a value worth protecting. Security measures are therefore not limited to the protection of a humanitarian organisation's staff, assets and operations but also the defence of its reputation and institutional interests.

The Predictability and Calculability of Danger

Moreover, juxtaposed to a "personal sense of security", described as a "subjective and therefore potentially misleading form of threat and risk assessment relying on one's personal impressions of a situation",[56] security management frameworks are depicted as tools capable of producing "objective" and "scientific" analyses, policies and procedures, thereby overcoming the propensity for human error. This is particularly true with regard to risk analyses. Conceptualised as a mathematical function, i.e. risk = likelihood (threat, vulnerability) x impact,[57] it is presumed that danger can be calculated through a methodical analysis coupled with the cross-referencing of variables. Whether articulated as numerical or categorical typologies, illustrating risk in such terms gives an impression of the precision, exactness and certainty of its measure, in sharp contrast with the uncertainty so rife in conflict situations.

People as Sources of Danger

Associated with this positivist approach, manuals such as the GPR 8 contribute to the discrediting of individual judgment and initiative. Whereas the awareness approach of the mid-1990s valued the individual and their capacity to adapt to new environments, the "management approach" tries to eliminate or minimise the role of the individual through the modelisation of security and risk. In doing so, field personnel become constructed both as threats to themselves and to others and, as a consequence, are subject to a form of disciplinary power or control limiting the scope of their actions and their forms of expression.

In addition, security management frameworks provide a particular vision of the countries where humanitarians operate. While NGO annual reports, publicity campaigns and websites display images of vulnerable, suffering populations in need, risk analyses and their resultant risk maps and lists of high-risk countries relay a frightening portrayal of these countries and their inhabitants. Host countries and even beneficiaries are presented as sources of risk and insecurity for humanitarian operations and their personnel. In contrast, aid workers are seen merely as "good people doing good work."[58] Coupled with this negative portrayal, field personnel are told to "[b]e aware and suspicious. Look for the unusual. [...] Presume that you may be a victim."[59] As such, manuals encourage humanitarians and NGO employees to scrutinise their operating environments through a lens of suspicion and fear.

Insecurity as a Technical Problem and the Expert as a Remedy

This view of populations in danger as dangerous populations is combined with an apolitical conception of security issues. The acceptance paradigm assumes that a humanitarian agency's security relies primarily on perception rather than on political transactions—that it suffices to be perceived as "good people doing good work" in the name of universal values. This denial of politics is well illustrated by recommendations concerning public communication, which is either viewed as a marketing tool to promote the moral and social value of humanitarian actors or, at the other end of the spectrum, as a potential source of danger.

Lastly, shunning politics goes hand in hand with the promotion of security management as an area of expertise. Manuals such as the GPR 8 participate in the transformation of security into a specialised knowledge and the monopolisation of that knowledge by a specific corporation of "professionals". As such, the GPR 8 functions as an "anti-politics machine", transforming inherently political decisions related to security into "technical solutions to technical problems."[60]

In summary, this corpus of humanitarian security manuals forms a coherent and reassuring narrative that can be resumed as follows: "The world is increasingly dangerous for humanitarian organizations, which are both legally and morally responsible for the security of their personnel. But these dangers can be overcome (and aid organisations can be protected from legal and reputational risks) through the objective measurement of risks, the rational planning of security strategy and the standardisation of aid workers' behaviours and public expression." The power of this narrative allows aid organisations to conceal the security dilemmas arising from operating in dangerous situations, while justifying the need for authoritarian control over their personnel in the name of security.

WHO BENEFITS FROM "DUTY OF CARE"?

Jonathan Edwards and Michaël Neuman

"I am somewhat worried that by elevating our duty of care obligations to a level that may meet liability standards in home societies we risk fundamentally sabotaging our operational mission."

MSF Operations Manager, 2015

Rooted in the common law legal system, the principle of duty of care is broadly defined as an employer's duty "to take reasonable steps to provide a safe system of work to avoid the risk of reasonably foreseeable injury, whether physical or psychiatric."[61] This approach dates back to nineteenth-century Britain when reaction to appalling rates of morbidity and mortality in factories and mines led to the introduction of a series of health and safety laws and regulations that included access to compensation for injured workers. This legal and regulatory framework advanced throughout the twentieth century, consolidating during the 1970s into the "workplace health and safety" regimes that wield such influence on societal understanding of risk and liability issues, particularly in English-speaking countries.[62] Similar provisions exist in continental Europe where they are embedded in the labour laws of various countries.[63] French civil labour law, for instance, stipulates that employers (French or otherwise) have the general obligation to ensure a safe working environment for their employees: "The employer shall take all the necessary measures to ensure the safety, and to protect the physical and mental health of workers."[64] Employers thus have the obligation to assess and manage any foreseeable risk. French case law has gone on to develop a broad interpretation of this obligation, regardless of the level of risk employees may be subject to.[65]

As for other high-risk occupations, laying out the practical implications of duty of care from the practitioner's perspective is particularly challenging, as, by definition, the act of providing relief in situations of conflict involves an exposure to risk. In 1997 and 2003, the NGO consortium People in Aid[66] set out a "Code of Best Practice" to define the employer's obligations under duty of care: briefing staff on the situation in the place they are to be assigned to, keeping records of work-related injuries, accidents and fatalities and performing regular reviews of security procedures. These norms in duty of care have now been widely adopted by aid agencies as standard[67] and feature regularly in discussions on best practices in human resources management for humanitarian organisations.[68] Yet the duty of care frame still raises key questions around the potential practical and legal implications, which need to be evaluated on a case-by-case basis as they depend as much on the contexts of intervention as on national legal frameworks.

While originally introduced into the aid sector as a good practice standard in human resource management, "duty of care" is increasingly considered from the legal and liability perspective. "Can you get sued?", a review conducted by Geneva-based think tank Security Management Initiative in 2011, examined international aid organisations (IAOs) with legal obligations under both common law jurisdictions and European strict liability and concluded that, despite a growing awareness of legal responsibilities towards staff, "serious gaps exist between legal requirements and current practice as to employer obligations."[69] More precisely, they point to a majority of the IAOs interviewed as lacking "a proper occupational health and safety protocol", 30 per cent any "institutionalised security management and reporting" and 66 per cent without a budget allocated expressly to security. Organisations that have not decided to consider security as a fully-fledged professional sector are thus deemed to be legally at fault. Drawing from recent legal cases in the commercial sector,[70] the authors also warn of the possible damages that could be awarded if judgments are made against organisations found to be in some way negligent. In the same vein, the authors, one of whom is specialised in employment law and personal injury law, urge aid organisations to seek legal advice, conduct routine in-depth risk analyses, and design and implement risk mitigation procedures. Though scarcely able to produce more than one case of judicial liability in the past thirty-five years,[71] unsurprisingly, the authors insist on the need to implement systems recommended by experts to analyse and mitigate risk.[72]

This approach, as the title "Can you get sued?" suggests, sets out as much to protect an organisation from liability risks as to protect an individual employee from danger. Opinions across the MSF movement still differ regarding the significance and implications of the ever-increasing focus on duty of care prevalent in Western society, and more particularly in the aid sector. Operational managers are more likely to highlight the risk of compromising MSF's operational scope through a narrow and bureaucratic understanding of the requirements of duty of care; board members from particularly litigious home countries are more sensitive to personal exposure to liability;[73] and human resources managers are principally concerned with the operational sustainability gains to be found in properly implemented HR policies that care for their employees (and not simply their security). The debates are many, reflecting the far-reaching and contradictory ambitions of the concept.

But there are signs within MSF of an increasing focus on the legal dimension of duty of care. For example, during the response to the Ebola emergency in 2014, several MSF sections introduced a page-and-a-half-long assumption of risk and acknowledgement of liability form to be signed by international staff prior to leaving for the field. It includes the following clause:

> I understand, acknowledge and accept that participation in an Ebola field mission, by its very nature, involves certain physical and health risks that cannot be eliminated regardless of the care taken to protect Ebola field mission staff. Those risks include the risk that I may contract Ebola. [...] I knowingly assume all such physical and health risks. [...] I understand that MSF is taking every precaution to protect me while I am participating in a Ebola field mission but that I am ultimately responsible for my health and my safety in the field.

The form ends with an "informed consent for medical treatment" clause, according to which staff "delegate to MSF [...] all power and authority" regarding potential medical treatment and management of care in the event that they contract or are suspected to have contracted Ebola during their assignment. This document is a manifest attempt to mitigate the threat of legal action. It makes clear that MSF has taken all necessary protection steps, thereby indicating that any contamination would be the responsibility of the contaminated person. Its introduction came within the somewhat exceptional context of an epidemic response suffused with a sense of danger for employees, their families and those around them that was deemed to be unprecedented. Nevertheless, it is hard to conclude that the sole objective of this expression of duty of care was to improve the safety of personnel; rather, it was a testimony to the progressively legal nature of the employee/employer relationship.

The pervasive interpretation of duty of care in terms of "institutional risk" is also found in the Volunteer Agreement that all volunteers employed by MSF's French section have to sign prior to departing on mission. In addition to an already well-detailed contract, under the terms of which the volunteer commits to share in MSF's Charter and "principles" and "acknowledges that he/she has been warned and is aware of the inherent risks linked to the mission allocated to him/her", one annex stipulates that the volunteer commits "to observe and abide by the security rules and guidelines established by MSF and its representatives [...] and to comply with them at all times". It is worth noting that this clause was recently reintroduced having been removed a few years ago when a number of staff members reacted negatively to it, finding it too prescriptive of their conduct. Partly a response by the management team to problems of misconduct, the reintroduction of this clause also reflects MSF's willingness to regulate behaviour as a means of ensuring strict adherence to risk mitigation procedures such as those recommended in the legal advice discussed above.

Looking at the key indicators identified by People in Aid to assess aid agencies' compliance with duty of care requirements in terms of security, it could be argued that MSF is a "responsible employer". How far this translates to meeting duty of care obligations in legal terms is a matter of dispute as, again, the complexities of managing the legal environments for an organisation with employees from dozens of countries are staggering. And yet another critical issue is the status of national staff. Current inequities in the relationship between MSF as an employer and its workforce—as highlighted recently through the different levels of access to healthcare and support provided to international and national staff working with Ebola patients—must be challenged.

If organisations do not find suitable solutions themselves, then they may find them imposed by others, as in the case of Irish Aid's "Guidelines for NGO Professional Safety & Security Risk Management", which aim to help "NGO partners to fulfil their duty of care responsibilities towards their own staff".[74] These standards recommend appropriate recruitment, training, risk assessment, consent, mitigation measures and legal health and safety compliance for all staff. Deriving their influence from their link to accreditation and funding eligibility from Irish Aid, this "guideline" approach may well be widely replicated by other donors and governments. This has yet to happen, but if it were to be broadly adopted the implications for humanitarian organisations could be significant.

So the challenge facing MSF and other such organisations is to first define their own vision of this somewhat nebulous concept of duty of care and then to establish the extent to which it is being achieved. An organisation-wide response to the question "what is your duty of care to your staff?" should not invoke an institutional risk mitigation approach, but leaving this issue to those managers closest to a mainstream and somewhat legalistic interpretation of duty of care, or to external regulators, risks doing exactly that.

PRACTICES

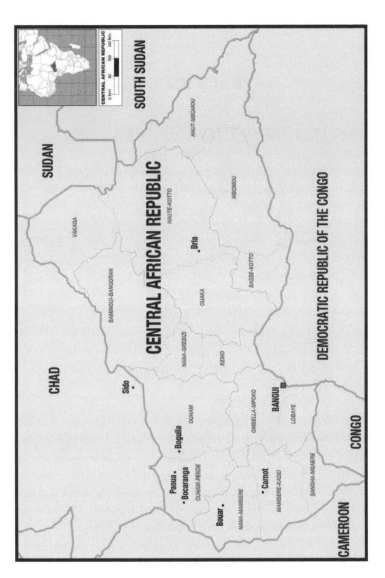

Map 1: Central African Republic

6

THE DUTY OF A HEAD OF MISSION

INTERVIEW WITH DELPHINE CHEDORGE,
MSF EMERGENCY COORDINATOR
IN CENTRAL AFRICAN REPUBLIC

Interviewed by
Michaël Neuman[1]

Landlocked Central African Republic (CAR) has a population of 4 million people and a wholly inadequate healthcare infrastructure. In terms of funding, the country ranks first for MSF-France and third for the MSF movement as a whole, after the Democratic Republic of Congo and South Sudan.[2] Also one of the most dangerous countries, four MSF employees have been killed in its conflicts since 2007. In 2014, 300 international and over 2,500 Central African staff members worked on some twenty medical projects.

MSF emergency coordinator Delphine Chedorge headed the French section's operations in CAR from January to December 2014. She spoke with Michaël Neuman about the everyday life of a head of mission in charge of team security. The interview is preceded by a summary of the recent events leading up to the bloodshed in CAR.

The 2013–2014 Crisis in the CAR

The CAR has experienced a cycle of violence unprecedented in its postcolonial history. In March 2013, an alliance of armed opposition movements, the Seleka, seized power and installed Michel Djotodia as president. During the months that followed, the new regime's violent attacks against the population and the previous government's forces led to the formation of local militias. The result of an alliance between village self-defence militias and members of the former national army, these so-called "anti-Balaka" groups echoed the population's mounting anger against a government increasingly perceived as "foreign" and "Muslim".[3]

Amid growing tensions and the fear of sectarian massacres, on 5 December 2013 the United Nations Security Council voted to dispatch an International Support Mission (known by the French acronym MISCA) to Central African Republic to re-establish state authority and protect civilians. MISCA was placed under the supervision of the African Union, with backing from French military operation "Sangaris". The same day, a large-scale offensive by anti-Balaka militias against Bangui failed to bring down the regime and resulted in the flight of ex-Seleka[4] rebels and the stepping-up of the international military deployment. After the anti-Balaka and some of the civilian population looted and committed massacres against Muslims living in Bangui, who had been left unprotected, the routed ex-Seleka launched an onslaught of unrestrained violence.[5]

With his back against the wall, President Djotodia gave into international pressure and resigned on 10 January 2014. However, the appointment of a transitional government did not restore the stability that had been hoped for. The ex-Seleka continued their bloody retreat toward the countries on CAR's north, east and west borders with anti-Balaka groups in hot pursuit. Meanwhile, the anti-Balaka encouraged and led massacres against Muslims forced to flee to neighbouring countries or the few enclaves within CAR protected by international forces. A retrospective mortality survey conducted in April 2014 by MSF among CAR refugees in Sido in Chad revealed that 8 per cent of those who had fled died between November 2013 and April 2014, with 91 per cent of these deaths attributed to violent acts committed during the campaign of persecution against Muslim minorities.

At the time of the attempted coup d'état of 5 December 2013, MSF's French section was running three projects in the country—primary and secondary healthcare programmes in Paoua sub-prefecture in the north-west, where it had been working since 2006, and paediatric services in Carnot and

Bria. In December, the section set up an emergency operation to care for the victims of the conflict, with particular focus on Bangui. The Spanish and Dutch sections were also working in CAR and were joined in early 2014 by the Swiss and Belgian sections.

Michaël Neuman: What was the situation when you first arrived in CAR?

Delphine Chedorge: My first assignment in CAR dates back to the summer of 2007. I've been back several times since, for three months in 2012, then for one year in early 2014. I started off as emergency coordinator and in April I became head of mission. The current conflict began in December 2012 and intensified after the Seleka took power in March 2013, which led to the collapse of the country's security forces. So in a sense, I "missed out" on just over a year of the conflict's progress. During the first few weeks I had a hard time getting a handle on the security situation. What's more, my knowledge of the country was very localised as it was centred on the north-west, where most of MSF-France's programmes have traditionally been concentrated. I took some time to get to grips with what was going elsewhere in the country. And, personally, I wasn't expecting such a violent sectarian conflict to break out.

What were the biggest security issues in Bangui when you arrived?

When I landed in Bangui in January 2014, there was lots of shooting in the city, including near the Hôpital Communautaire, where we were treating the wounded, and our living quarters and offices. Everyone was in the same neighbourhood, right in the middle of an urban war.

It was also very difficult to get to the Muslim enclaves and neighbourhoods. In January and February we made several attempts to fetch casualties from so-called PK12 district where groups of Muslims wanting to flee had assembled and were under constant attack from particularly unpredictable militiamen. PK12 was also notable for its close proximity to an ex-Seleka camp. International forces were stationed there to protect civilians and the ex-Seleka, which created a really tense atmosphere. Sometimes we met with so much hostility we had to turn back.

National and international staff alike were highly exposed to danger. They often had to negotiate with armed, aggressive individuals entering the hospital to look for a particular patient or demanding to be treated ahead of the others. They witnessed first-hand the ferocity of the violence and its consequences in the numbers of casualties and types of wounds requiring treatment. Because of fighting nearby, the hospital team repeatedly had to seek shelter in the bulletproof operating theatre—which the in-patient tents weren't. Staff members were experiencing high levels of physical and mental fatigue. Nobody was hurt, but the risk was high. No one asked to leave, which would've been perfectly understandable. We brought in psychiatrists and psychologists to debrief the teams.

What steps did you take to reduce the personnel's exposure to danger?

When I first arrived, the head office security focal point was already there helping the teams to protect themselves, for example, from stray bullets entering houses, which had happened several times since December. He set up safe rooms that the staff used when the fighting was close-by. The hospital team were also afraid of staying at the hospital, especially overnight. So we decided that they would only work there from 8am to 4pm. We had to assume responsibility for patients having less access to medical treatment.

We sometimes designed our activities in a way we thought would increase our security while trying to establish more trust with armed groups and civilians (it was sometimes hard to distinguish between the two). For example, while treating victims of the violence that occurred in the Fatima neighbourhood in May and June and which caused fifteen to twenty casualties among the displaced population, we also ran mobile clinics in neighbouring Christian districts. Obviously, these clinics did serve a useful medical purpose—such as treating infantile malaria—but the primary motivation was to avoid being accused of working only with Muslims, even if our health centre in mainly Muslim PK5 district did, of course, provide care for Christians as well.

We also worked hard on getting information. The primary sources were the national staff, most of whom I had known for a long time. They described to me what was happening in the various districts, the groups, their weapons, what they were saying, the rumours and threats they were spreading. They also helped me identify which streets were dangerous. I wasn't familiar with Bangui's roads because MSF had no programmes there. We had to make a micro-political analysis of the dynamics in each of the city's districts. We drove all over the city observing the situation. We used a driver who said he felt comfortable driving around certain neighbourhoods and he provided a running commentary on what was going on.

We worked quite well with the other MSF sections present in Bangui. One had established a working relationship with ex-Seleka while another had more recent ties with anti-Balaka groups due to their work in the M'Poko displaced persons camp.[6] During the early days of my assignment, we were fairly dependent on these contacts. We worked on the basis of trust—let's say, not blind, but informed trust. It was hard for me, but it made sense. There were only so many contacts I could handle. Beginning in April, I regained control of contacts in cooperation with my colleagues from the other sections.

Could you also rely on outside information, from journalists and other NGOs working in the country?

Our information mainly came from three networks: missionaries, Ministry of Health medical staff and national Red Cross staff. All were very active in protecting civilians or providing relief when the fighting was at its most intense. We were also in regular contact with old acquaintances—all kinds of political officials, former rebels and district leaders. In addition, the person who had the job of head of mission when I arrived had developed her own network of officials working for some of the other NGOs operating in CAR and we were also in contact with several UN agencies and some of their staff.

At the beginning, there were few organisations delivering aid and travelling around the city and the rest of the country. The United Nations and the French army, followed by the European force EUFOR and later INSO (an NGO specifically responsible for security), gradually set up systems to provide information—usually incomplete and unreliable—to humanitarian organisations. The organisations responsible for keeping others from harm—which is more especially the military's job—would say "avoid going here or there" or "take an armed escort". There was some value in giving their advice serious consideration, but it was also important to maintain our decision-making autonomy. In the final analysis, and this was instructive, it was less the information itself (sometimes no more than rumours with no attempt at objectivity) than what it taught us about how much we could trust those providing the information and what they were willing or not willing to share.

Concerning the national staff, were there any specific security issues or requests?

Most of the Central African staff in Bangui lived in neighbourhoods severely affected by the conflict and they were very afraid of moving around the city. In December 2013, many of them stopped coming to the office. Coordination had set up a shuttle system to pick them up. This system closed down in early February 2014 as there was much less fighting in the city and taxis were running again. Despite this, employees regularly stayed overnight in our offices and houses because they couldn't get home. As of September, being identified as an MSF employee no longer afforded protection and actually posed more of a risk, as employed people have money. Because of the gang culture invading Bangui, their security was jeopardised far more than ours. And, even more dramatically, all our Muslim employees had left the city, and most of them probably the country. We still don't know what's happened to many of them.

What were the main security problems outside Bangui?

Until October, we were occasionally able to travel by road in the interior of the country, despite a number of incidents. Of course, NGO and UN employees were sometimes targeted, but it was more for the equipment. In January 2014, a group of ex-Seleka stole a car from us. They stopped us, explained they needed a car for a day or two, took away our radio and MSF stickers and unloaded the car. We got it back after putting pressure on their commanders. The car had been used in combat. The same thing happened when an anti-Balaka group "confiscated" our truck and its crew before returning it a few days later. The truck was also used in combat. This type of "respect", albeit relative, gradually disappeared over the course of the year. The risk was greatest on the roads, with anti-Balaka roadblocks manned by drunk, drugged-up fighters with no real chain of command. We had to limit travel by road and hire an extra plane to relieve staff and supply our programmes. This seemed to be the only option that would allow us to work in security conditions that we deemed acceptable. This decision was the subject of regular and exhausting discussions with head office who felt that the plane cost too much.

During this period, MSF-France was working in three locations, in Paoua in the north-west, Carnot in the west and Bria in the east. How did the security situation in these three areas evolve over time?

We were expecting Bria and Paoua to be the most vulnerable because they had been affected by the conflicts of the early 2000s. But Carnot ended up suffering the worst violence. There were numerous clashes between civilians, anti-Balaka, ex-Seleka and then Cameroonian MISCA forces, who were acting as a buffer between, on the one hand, the anti-Balaka militias and Carnot's inhabitants, and on the other, Muslims trapped in the enclave who had barricaded themselves inside the church. The team witnessed massacres of Muslims on several occasions, especially in January, when we had to call on Cameroonian MISCA forces based a few hours away by road to the north to intervene to prevent Muslims being driven out of their homes and killed.

Displaced Muslims attempting to get medical treatment were at great risk and many refused to go to hospitals because of the extreme danger involved in getting to them. However, the team were able to negotiate with the anti-Bal-aka militias and some inhabitants a safe passage for the MSF ambulance transporting wounded Muslims and MISCA soldiers so they could be evacuated by plane to Bangui.

After clashes between international forces and anti-Balaka, in July 2014 a Fula patient was lynched inside Carnot hospital. This was one of the most serious incidents that had ever occurred in one of MSF-France's programmes. You then began a "mobilisation campaign"—first local, then national—calling for the protection of healthcare facilities. What were you hoping to achieve with public statements about a security incident?

We probably should have done it sooner because we realised that some of the health workers were in fact not surprised that sectarian groups were settling accounts inside a health facility. Our message was: the hospital provides care for everyone and we cannot tolerate any violence; otherwise, we'll have to leave. The team went to ask all the local health and political authorities, armed groups, local people and neighbourhood leaders to get all their contacts to spread the message that this was not normal. We succeeded in getting the message through.

Then, when we talked with the team and the other sections of MSF, we realised that what had happened in Carnot could happen anywhere. That's why we decided on a national campaign, which included other MSF sites. We used posters and radio broadcasts to call for the protection of our medical activities.

Wasn't it somewhat futile to call for the protection of health facilities on the basis of humanitarian principles?

It doesn't hurt to use these magic words, so long as they're followed up with a conversation and much more tangible negotiation. When an incident occurs, we try to determine the cause of the problem and our role in it. We also try to figure out how we can continue operating and providing relief in the particular environment. In the case of Carnot, it was in everyone's interests that we stay. But our communications were not limited to the campaign. The local press in CAR published all public statements made in response to security incidents. Despite the lack of public reaction from politicians, some of our contacts did call us—even if only to see how we were coping. By speaking out, we could also counter government rhetoric about the supposed "normalisation" of the situation, which Central African and international officials (with

France taking the lead) began claiming in late 2014. In view of the increasing number of robberies at homes and offices belonging to other MSF sections operating in the country, attacks on vehicles on roads, extortion and the seizure of our transporters' trucks, it was important to make a point.

Central African Republic is where MSF-France's last international volunteer was killed. It was in June 2007 and the victim was Elsa Serfass, a logistician with the Paoua programme. You first worked in CAR in the days and weeks following this tragic event. Did this incident affect the way you managed security during your most recent assignment?

My greatest and most constant fear was losing a member of our team. I used to bring up Elsa's death in my briefings with volunteers. Telling the story provided an opportunity to remind them about all the weapons that were circulating and the state of chaos in the country. This was important because, even in 2014 during a time of extreme violence, as soon as the situation calmed down for a few days, some team members could be quick to forget that we were working in a dangerous country. You also have to be honest with people coming to a programme and give them specific examples, such as murder, rape and lynching of patients.

I believe it is unacceptable to hide serious incidents from people arriving in the field. Even I found myself without information about a number of serious incidents—including sexual assaults—against colleagues in other sections. This led to some tense conversations. Managers sometimes tend to withhold information because they want to protect the dignity of the victims, but this information is vital to assessing the shifting nature of the risks teams are exposed to.

And, there's a risk of the violence becoming trivialised. People immersed in a dangerous environment where incidents are commonplace can become inured to danger and no longer react to it because they end up seeing exposure to violence as the norm.

What were the circumstances that led you to suspend operations or evacuate staff during your assignment?

In 2014, when we thought there might be a significant deterioration in the situation, we carried out several preventive evacuations to reduce exposure to danger. For example, during the violence that took place in Bangui in October, we decided to evacuate twenty-four people by road and boat to three neighbouring countries over three days. And then there was the attack against

Boguila hospital in April, which left nineteen people dead, including three of MSF-Holland's national staff. We had lots of discussions with the heads of mission of the five sections working in CAR about how we should respond. There were two opposing opinions. The first advocated closing all projects in the country for a set period of time in the slim hope that such an extreme decision would provoke a reaction from the armed groups. The second, more moderate, opinion, mainly supported by MSF-Holland's head of mission, called for evacuating just the international personnel and staff relocated[7] from Boguila. In the end, we chose the more minimal option of limiting care to emergency cases across all programmes for one week. An exception was made for Boguila, where international and relocated employees were withdrawn for a longer period and replaced with spasmodic visits. We found out who was responsible for the killings—a leader of an ex-Seleka group. But we didn't speak out and release this information to the public. Instead, we complained to his superiors and waited to see what they would do. But to no avail as he's still at large.

MSF's operations in Paoua ended up being suspended for the longest period, even though the area had been the least affected by the war. How do you explain that?

In August, our Central African employees began making a series of demands, which they backed up with a strike. They wanted salary increases and transport allowances. We didn't agree to these demands so they decided to call a day of strike, while maintaining minimum service. During the strike, which took place in September, picket lines were set up and some employees who wanted to continue working were seriously threatened. The local authorities who had agreed to act as mediators were accused of being traitors, which raised the question of whether we could continue to operate. The team was finally evacuated in December after international staff began receiving death threats. They made a gradual return, but only at the very end of the year.

MSF has been working in Paoua since 2006. How would you explain this deterioration?

The first factor has to do with a context specific to Central African Republic, the deteriorating labour relations resulting from the many years of violence in the region and the absence of State representatives and local government mediators—and all this against the backdrop of an economic crisis. Other organisations also had to deal with very difficult labour conflicts. The second factor is internal to MSF. During the year, five people had successively held the position of project coordinator in Paoua and this lack of continuity definitely impacted our ability to make a clear assessment of the worsening situation, particularly regarding labour issues. What's more, we were taken up with the other programmes because we felt their teams were at much greater risk so, for sure, the coordination team didn't monitor the situation closely enough.

In general, how much autonomy do project coordinators have to assess and handle security?

It depends on the person and how our relationship develops. Not everyone has the same amount of experience or the same ability to analyse the situation they find themselves in. For example, when I consider the explanations and precautions aren't sufficiently convincing to justify a journey, I can refuse to give my authorisation. When you feel that your team leader has a handle on all this, you can give more autonomy.

We partially delegated the security of one team to another organisation: Catholic missionaries, as it happens. This is a very rare occurrence at MSF nowadays. For a few days in late January 2014, we left a small two-person team—an anaesthetist and a surgeon—in Bossemptele to the north-west of Bangui with no car or means of communication. This was at the time the ex-Seleka were taking flight and the anti-Balaka were carrying out violent reprisals against the town's Muslims, causing many casualties. Wounds were becoming infected because the Central African doctor at the missionary hospital was out of the necessary supplies. So we decided to send two people to give them a hand.

This was a really specific situation. The Catholic mission was actively defending and helping Muslims in the area, the priest was accustomed to interacting with all of the armed groups, and there were missionary nuns there too. The mission compound was relatively well protected. I left the team there without a car. At the time, having a well-maintained MSF car would have attracted the militias' attention, so not having one was actually safer. The team was almost invisible, but nevertheless, all the political and military groups were aware they were there; we didn't act surreptitiously.

In Central African Republic as in other places, MSF has in recent years decided to ban some volunteers from working in certain programmes on the basis of their nationality and the colour of their skin. How did we get to this?

We decided to do this in two cases. In April 2014, a logistician was attacked in Bria for being white and French. French Sangaris forces present in the area were seen as taking sides against the Muslims and we were at risk of being associated with them. The first step we took was to pull out the volunteer. Then we decided to stop assigning white people there at all, since they might have been thought to be French. We soon realised that this was an isolated incident; the perpetrator had been upset and angry because his son has been killed in the fighting. And, in fact, lots of people had jumped in and defended the logistician.

Nevertheless, there could have been more cases like that, so, after talking with the team, for several months we kept to our decision. Considering our overall operational volume and the number of international staff in the country, we were simply making our jobs easier. But we didn't prevent visits by the coordination team working out of Bangui. These increased, to such an extent that the restriction lost its meaning. We definitely could have brought white Western staff back in faster.

Then came the issue of staff with Muslim backgrounds. To avoid any problems, we adopted a super-pragmatic position because we thought that North Africans would be seen as white by the anti-Balaka. As for the Africans, some of them changed their first names to less Muslim-sounding ones. This was left up to each individual. On the other hand, I myself refused to appoint a Malian Tuareg as deputy head of mission because the nature of his job would have meant showing his face as he moved around Bangui, which would have posed too much of a risk.

Among the issues relating to security in Central Africa, the extent of MSF's exposure was a major concern. Many people felt there were too many staff on the ground: 300 international employees, eighty of them in the French section alone, and 2,500 national employees in all MSF sections. What was your position on this issue?

You have to remember that Bangui is the most dangerous city in CAR and it's where the coordination team is located. It's also the city with the largest team. If you add the employees working at the hospital and our health centre in PK5 to the coordination team, there can sometimes be over forty-five international employees.

What's more, head office's decision to reduce operations in order to limit our exposure to danger contradicted their policy of deploying "first assignments" [or "first missions", to use NGO-speak] to the field. In an environment that was unstable at best, and frankly dangerous most of the time, jobs were created to meet the need to train new volunteers rather than immediate operational requirements. It was completely contradictory and done without my agreement. In Paoua, for example, this was the case of two volunteers out of a total of eight and, after the violence that occurred in Bangui in October, I had to get them out via Chad in dangerous conditions.

At the beginning of our interview, you mentioned the role of the security focal point—an innovation for the French section instituted in 2013. The focal point's appointment coincided with the operation department's introduction of systematised "security management tools", such as the risk assessment matrix and the system used to record and file information on security incidents known as "SINDY". What do you think of these measures?

The logbook for recording incidents occurring in the areas where we operate, the guides, briefings and emergency public statements issued after incidents— all these were nothing new. The security focal point helped us make the team aware of the security environment and contributed to briefings, particularly with the logisticians tasked with setting up security measures (communications, safe rooms and tracking travel). This aspect was useful. Then, when he returned to head office in Paris, he insisted that we keep the SINDY database up-to-date. SINDY is a centralised system for filing reports on security incidents affecting only MSF.[8] This we disagreed about because I didn't feel it was of direct benefit to the field. We already had logbooks and incident registers for recording important events to be taken into account in analysing the security environment. I'm sure it's useful for MSF as an institution to keep a database of reports of the most serious incidents but, given that we were already very busy, I didn't think it was necessary to do head office's secretarial work. What is important is working with the team on managing incidents and sharing the information with the other sections. And the other danger with using SINDY in the field is that people will only see the problem from the MSF perspective and overlook incidents affecting other agencies.

To get back to the risk assessment, isn't there something scary about making an exhaustive list of the threats you might be facing?

Yes, I ask myself that question. But in my experience, when I use the risk assessment during briefings I've noticed that the people I'm talking with become calmer and more focused as the conversation goes on. Their eyes are opened and they become more aware of their environment. In the end, after these conversations, people feel prepared and confident because they know the situation has been well thought out.

The idea is for people to be on their guard. There needs to be a balance between trivialising and exaggerating the risk.

At MSF and other organisations, there's a certain amount of protest against the growing number of security rules in the field. One of your head of mission colleagues who spent a few weeks in Bangui said that "the curfew rules treat volunteers like children and encourage them to flout the rules".

Of course this happens; it's a natural consequence of rules. But the volunteers didn't seem particularly reluctant to comply with them. When they did flout them, it was in a way that didn't put them at too much risk. That's what we ask of people: when you break a rule, make sure you know why and how. If we need to, we'll talk it through again and, if necessary, we'll change it.

For example, when you ban your teams from going to the flea market in Bangui, is it because you worry there might be be serious problems or is it because you might have to deal with the theft of a careless volunteer's bag?

What actually happened was that ordinary petty thieves got themselves grenades and were more and more violent. Also, you don't manage forty international staff the same way you manage ten; you can't talk to each one, look into every issue, etc. We definitely wouldn't have had the same rules if there'd been five or ten of us in Bangui, but we were forty to fifty. It also explains something that was occasionally contested. When the security situation in town settled down enough to allow volunteers to go out, different curfew hours for weekdays (9pm) and weekends (10pm) were introduced. I never thought the city was less dangerous at the weekend. On the other hand, from a personal point of view, a simple question of fatigue, I couldn't allow myself to be on call every evening of the week to deal with a car stopped at a police checkpoint on the way back from a restaurant. I was okay with being available an hour later at the weekend in case of problems so they could have more freedom. It's a shame the teams couldn't manage small incidents like these without outside help but it wasn't always the case. I was making life easier with these rules. They were geared more toward management of human resources than security management.

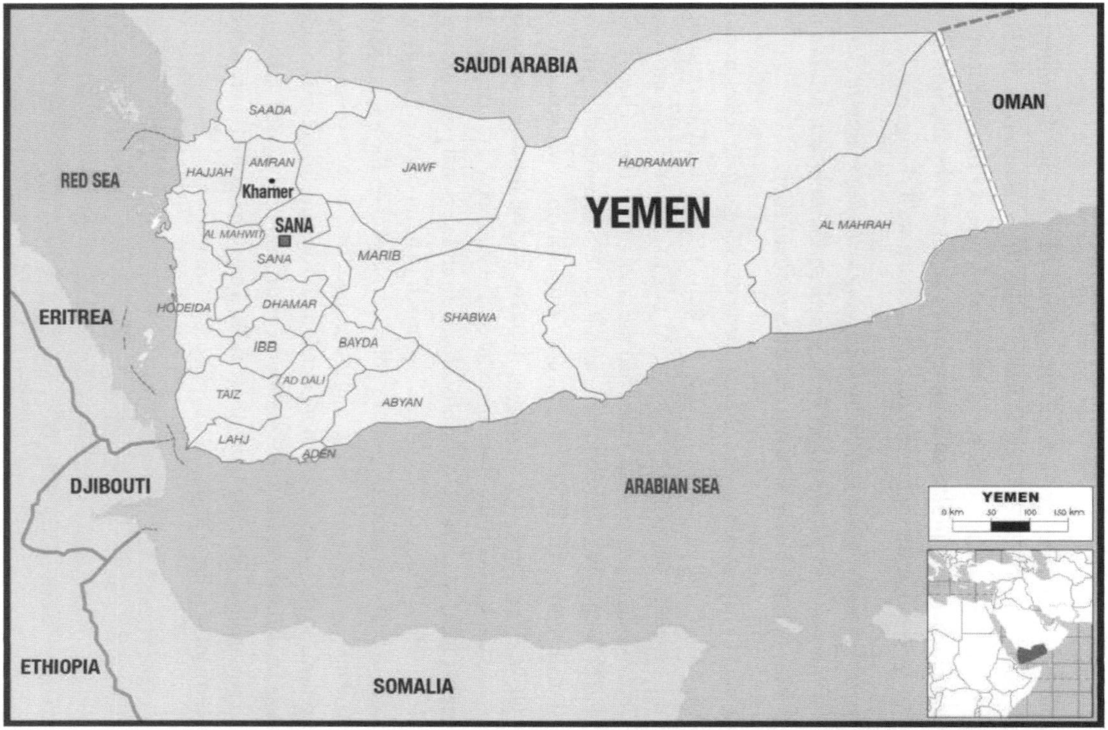
SAUDI ARABIA
OMAN
SAADA
HAJJAH
AMRAN
Khamer
JAWF
HADRAMAWT
YEMEN
AL MAHRAH
RED SEA
SANA
AL MAHWIT
SANA
MARIB
HODEIDA
DHAMAR
SHABWA
ERITREA
IBB
BAYDA
AD DALI
TAIZ
ABYAN
LAHJ
ADEN
DJIBOUTI
ARABIAN SEA
YEMEN
0 km
50
100
150 km
ETHIOPIA
SOMALIA

Map 2: Yemen

THE CASE OF "DANGEROUS PATIENTS" IN YEMEN'S GOVERNORATE OF AMRAN[9]

Michaël Neuman

"I would not want to be a doctor here."[10]

Already in 2010, well before Yemen became engulfed in all-out war between Houthi rebels and factions supported by Saudi Arabia in 2015, national and international staff working in MSF projects in Amran Governorate[11] viewed the situation as highly dangerous.

Khamer, where MSF has been in charge since 2011 of all the hospital's departments with the exception of the Ministry of Health-run outpatient Department (OPD), had been a peaceful town where international personnel were free to walk around—except at night, because of stray dogs. However, during the period from 17 April 2010 to 15 June 2013, MSF project coordinators in Khamer and in the nearby town of Huth, recorded twenty-three security incidents, none of which involved the death or kidnapping of any MSF employees. Verbal threats were a daily occurrence and being threatened at gunpoint was commonplace, as were shootings in the hospital compound and car-jackings. International employees were not usually affected, while Yemeni medical personnel working in the emergency room (ER) were more exposed than staff in the inpatient department (IPD). The most serious incident had been a revenge killing in 2011 that resulted in a patient's death at the hospital.

Such incidents led several Yemeni doctors to leave the projects. In 2012 alone, one surgeon left after being verbally threatened by the relative of a patient he had operated on, a doctor after being forced at gunpoint to treat a patient, and a third after he was slapped. A local doctor interviewed in 2013 commented: "There is a 20 per cent chance I get killed in the hospital, 80 per cent chance I stay safe."

This situation prompted the programme manager for Yemen to request an investigation into the logics of violence and the reactions to this violence of MSF and Ministry of Health staff. Conducted in July 2013, the investigation was based on interviews with patients, personnel and local authorities, mission archives and a review of pertinent social science literature on Yemen. Its main findings are presented below.

"Some Patients are Dangerous, We Know It."[12] *Referring Patients for Security Reasons*

In interviews, most Yemeni and international doctors tended to blame the insecurity on the lack of education of patients and their families and an "archaic tribal system living off the lack of strict regulation of government allowing any member of a tribe to do whatever he wants."[13] People from villages outside Khamer—the primary target population of the project—were perceived to be the main troublemakers. The doctors recognised that this perception influenced their medical practices, as one of them explained:

> When patients come from communities with whom we've had problems, it bloats, and then, the therapeutic decision has no longer any medical and scientific rationality. It is quite common to hear comments such as: 'this one is from this family', 'he is the son of that one', 'he comes from this region', etc. It has a significant impact.[14]

In fact, it was common for patients with alleged "dangerous profiles" to be referred to other medical facilities in Amran or Sanaa, even if their medical conditions did not warrant it. There was very little disagreement among Yemeni and international staff that, "if there is a security risk, it is better to refer."[15] In some cases, the decision was at the discretion of the night supervisor, a non-medical staff member who "knows everything and everybody."[16]

"Promises Are Not Followed by Acts."[17] *Dealing With the Sheikhs*

When a serious incident occurred, MSF frequently reacted by seeking the mediation of local tribal authorities[18] and sometimes suspended its activities to put pressure on them and their tribes. In most cases, after a period of suspension varying from one day to six months, mediation was successfully concluded, compensation paid—money, cows, or guns—and victims apologised to by culprits in a gathering of local leaders. This reactive approach to insecurity was criticised by some staff members for its ineffectiveness. Given that doctors could expect little protection from the various local institutions, staff demanded that MSF play a more assertive role in ensuring safety. A Yemeni doctor formerly employed by MSF commented:

> The only thing we've been doing lately is incident, apology ceremony, incident, apology ceremony, incident, etc. We have to think about it in a different way.

The international team seemed to believe that the sheikhs were all powerful, if only the right one could be identified. As a member of the international team said, "He can do whatever he wants with his people". However, some academics question this assertion, echoing the view of many Yemeni staff. As political scientist Laurent Bonnefoy explains, it is unreasonable to expect the sheikhs to prevent violence from occurring. Controlling violence in North Yemen is based first and foremost on "mitigation" and "regulation", rather than on "prevention", in an effort to ensure that conflicts do not get blown out of proportion and stay contained within acceptable limits.[19]

"Doctors are Parasites which Live on Human Blood."[20]

MSF's reaction to the violence appeared to overlook as a source of tension the poor relationship between doctors and patients. Generally speaking, Yemeni doctors appeared to suffer from a very poor image, as illustrated by an article published in *National Yemen* in July 2012 entitled "Yemeni doctors cause more harm than good":

> Thousands of Yemenis fall victim to medical errors at the hands of doctors, whose unearned and undeserved titles and certificates are the only things which connect them with the practice of medicine. (...) Many Yemenis have expressed their dissatisfaction with Yemeni doctors, who they say are not good at their jobs and have transformed their sacred profession into a way to earn money. Many have gone so far as to liken doctors to "parasites" which live on human blood.[21]

Some aspects of the operational set-up appear to have further exacerbated the general distrust. Lack of clarity in ER admission criteria was often mentioned as a factor of tension by both medical staff and patients. The ER saw around half of the total number of patients who arrived in triage, between 1,500 and 2,500 a month, while the other half were referred to the Ministry of Health's OPD, run by three doctors from the former Soviet Union, where services were not provided free of charge.

Many patients refused to be referred to the OPD and exerted pressure on medical staff to be treated by MSF. As one interviewee explained, "the more vocal the patients are, the better chances they get to be seen by the MSF doctor." Many people viewed this medically unjustified discrimination as the source of most of the problems encountered by the hospital's employees, and this was without taking into account, as a Yemeni MSF doctor explained, "our watchmen, our staff, nurses, nurses' assistants, they are taking their friends, their relatives to treat them. Sometimes we, the doctors, refuse, and sometimes, we don't."

Some patients did not understand why MSF delivered mostly emergency services and not, for example, care for chronic diseases and non-urgent surgery,[22] nor why they would be or needed to be referred to other facilities where they would have to pay. Routine profiling of patients by doctors according to where they came from and their family and tribal affiliations added to the tension. What's the point of having a hospital if it cannot be accessed?

The layout of the hospital also contributed to tension in and around the maternity ward.

> Part of the problem is that there is no waiting room in the maternity—the building is too small. So the families generally wait outside while the women are in labour. Sometimes it can last for hours, during which the family are left in the dark, uninformed about how things are going if the midwife in charge does not take the time to come out and talk to the families.[23]

Brief analysis of the incidents MSF staff encountered revealed their extreme diversity, as much in origin as in manifestation. Ultimately, the issues confronted by MSF in Amran were framed, for the most part, within a demand wholly comparable to that experienced by MSF and health professionals in hospitals all over the world: a quality relationship between patients and health personnel. At the hospital in Khamer, MSF operated in a setting where this expectation may have conflicted with the reality on the ground, given that the high level of violence in the region appeared to be generally socially accepted and that intimidation is integral to social regulation there. The investigation revealed that, while humanitarian organisations do not have to see themselves as passive victims, neither do they have to view Yemeni patients as inherently dangerous.

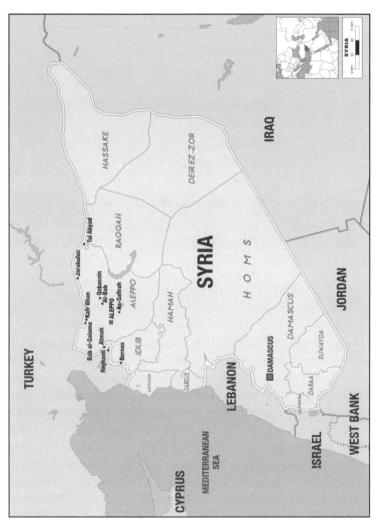

Map 3: Syria

7

QABASSIN, SYRIA

SECURITY ISSUES AND PRACTICES IN AN MSF MISSION IN THE LAND OF JIHAD

Judith Soussan[1]

On 11 May 2013, the coordinator of the Qabassin project sent an email to the coordination team in Turkey announcing the opening of the MSF hospital that very morning. He summed up with a downbeat "so far so good." He was certainly being modest, for there was much to be proud of. This was the first hospital set up by an NGO and with international staff to be located deep inside Syrian opposition-held territory rather than along the Turkish border like MSF's other projects: the hospitals in Atmah (MSF-France), a few kilometres as the crow flies from the coordination team's base in Reyhanli in Turkey, Bab al-Salama (MSF-Spain), Bernas (MSF-Belgium) and Tal Abyad (MSF-Holland). It had taken six weeks of extensive refurbishment to turn an empty building into a clean and well-equipped facility with surgery and maternity units, an emergency room and a twenty-five-bed inpatient department.

However, the opening of the Qabassin hospital, a small but significant event, did not get the attention it deserved. A bomb exploded the same day in Reyhanli, killing fifty-one people and injuring over 150, while the previous day armed men in Atmah verbally attacked and threatened to kill a Swedish MSF staff member they accused of spying. He then had to appear before a local Islamic court. In comparison, Qabassin seemed almost a haven of peace and the members of the team, all newly arrived and enjoying a quiet life during their time off, walking around the town, visiting the market and receiving invitations to take tea, had trouble taking the coordination team's calls for vigilance seriously. "They were too relaxed, they'd forgotten where they were," recalls the head of mission at the time.

This chapter tells the story of the Qabassin mission from the security perspective. It examines the perceptions and practices of the team in the field (starting with the field coordinators, who came and went at a rapid pace) and the coordination team in Turkey, with whom they were in permanent contact.[2] How did these people analyse their situation, the prevailing risks and events as they unfolded? What behaviours did they adopt in the face of danger—from the rules and procedures (introduced, modified or forgotten) to the various strategies designed to "reduce exposure" and "improve acceptance" (to use current parlance)? This chapter will pay particular attention to moments when disagreements arose, during which people's often complex definitions of the word "security" were revealed and came into conflict.[3]

Finding the Right Role in the War (Mid-2011 to Early 2013)

Exploration (How to Find Protection from Bombs?)

With the organisation's first attempts to take action in Syria in mid-2011, MSF-France's approach toward its operational positioning took the form of a common dilemma—how to operate within the context of the Syrian civil war and reach out as much as possible to its victims, without exposing teams to excessive risks or compromising quality of care.

It took the emergency desk team a lot of patience, several false starts, exploratory missions that failed to lead anywhere because the risks were considered too high, and finally a few pivotal encounters for MSF-France to open its first project in Atmah in June 2012. MSF was, as it's now called, "embedded", as the hospital and house where the international staff were accommodated and their security were all provided by a highly influential Atmah public figure, who was also a doctor and a member of one of the local Free Syrian Army (FSA) brigades. The many months of patient strategising and exploration in an environment where foreigners were strongly suspected of spying resulted in the watchwords: keep a low profile.

The Atmah project now open, MSF started to look for ways to reach out to areas more directly impacted by the conflict. Those behind the Syria programme had their eyes firmly fixed on Aleppo, a city split into a government zone and a constantly bombed FSA zone. But after an exploratory mission in August 2012, operations managers in Paris deemed it too dangerous and rejected the idea of sending in international staff, especially in light of the loyalist force's targeting of field hospitals.[4] Two further attempts to deploy operations failed. In October 2012, a hospital project set up in partnership with some Syrian doctors in Kafr Ghan near the Turkish border had to close three weeks after opening due to fundamental differences between MSF and the Syrians on how to run the hospital. Then MSF turned to Al-Bab, a city with 130,000 inhabitants situated some thirty kilometres from Aleppo along the route used to evacuate casualties. The project was well advanced when, in January 2013, the town was repeatedly bombed and the coordination team evacuated the project team to Turkey. In the words of the head of mission: "I told them, 'we're in the same situation as the Syrians, we're not protected. So we need to find a safer place.'"[5]

The database he had compiled showed that, out of all the places in a ten-kilometre radius around Al-Bab, the town of Qabassin had never been shelled. The team had also heard that its population of 20,000 Arabs and Kurds included a not insignificant proportion of people who backed the regime. And, unlike Atmah, where black-clad foreign Islamists paraded in their pickups, there was no visible armed presence. This was why, so it was said, Qabassin was untouched by the turmoil among opposition groups and bombing by pro-regime forces. On 27 January, the day after they were evacuated, two members of the small team decided to go to the town.

Opening the Project (How to Gain Acceptance?)

They carried on the work of identifying and meeting with key contacts initiated during the two months spent in Al-Bab. In addition to members of prominent families, they had met with representatives of nascent revolutionary institutions—the civilian-run local council, whose responsibilities included health, and the Islamic court, which handled justice and policing. The project coordinator had also established contact with representatives from local politico-military groups, including brigades affiliated with the FSA and Islamist groups such as Al-Qaeda affiliates Ahrar al-Sham and Jabhat al-Nusra. While maintaining these contacts in Al-Bab, they became acquainted with the small world of Qabassin. They met with influential local leaders, some of them also members of the local town council (there was no Islamic court as yet), as well as representatives of the Kurdish party affiliated to the Kurdistan Workers' Party (PKK).[6] "Tea. I drank a lot of tea during this period," recalls the project coordinator with a smile.

The team driving the Qabassin project wanted to do things differently to Atmah (not to rely on a protector) and to the failed Kafr Ghan project (to avoid co-management). The hospital was to be "100 per cent MSF." In terms of activities, however, the project was similar to the others, with surgery the focus to provide treatment to casualties evacuated from Aleppo via Al-Bab. The decision was also taken to offer general medical treatment and surgery to local people, a decision that, according to documents written at the time, met two essentially tactical objectives. First, to avoid appearing as a hospital for fighters, thus minimising the risk of being targeted for bombardment by the regime. Second, to gain better "acceptance by the community"[7] by allaying any possible concerns about the risks stemming from setting up a hospital in the town and offering services that people would probably need. The other major feature of the project would be to identify small medical facilities closer to the combat zone (including in Aleppo, which the organisation was not giving up on) that MSF could support as the situation evolved on the ground. These outreach activities would also enable MSF to channel sick and wounded to the hospital in Qabassin while monitoring needs engendered by local politico-military developments.

As preparations were underway, the team wrote an in-depth analysis of the risks and detailed the security rules. According to the Security Guidelines approved in March 2013, the main risks in Qabassin related to road traffic and the "psychological impact", i.e. stress.[8] In addition to these "high" probability dangers, bombing and crossfire were classified as "medium", and chemical weapons as "low to medium". The risk of kidnap—despite the abduction in Atmah on 13 March of two members of NGO ACTED—was described as low, "as we are well-known and well-accepted within the community."[9]

The security rules included standard procedures, for example relating to travel: in a car, wearing a seatbelt, carrying identity documents, leaving the Syrian driver to handle interactions with people manning checkpoints, and on foot, writing down destinations on the board used to keep track of where staff are going, and not walking alone or at night. But, a number of very strict and detailed rules governing personal behaviour were also laid down:

1. *Behaving appropriately towards staff/local people* is the very first security rule. Do not shout or address people aggressively (…) *No flirting/sexual relations between international/national [staff]*. 2. Laughing out loud can give the impression of being

drunk. (...) 4. *NO PHYSICAL CONTACT WHATSOEVER* between men and women (no hand-shaking, etc.). (...) *Do not take ANY photos* as people may think we are spies/journalists.[10]

Women must not smoke in public (...) Alcohol, illicit drugs and marijuana must not be taken or even discussed with Syrians. Do not discuss politics or religion. Dress appropriately outside the hospital at all times (men: no shorts, women: cover the head, arms, and legs no tight-fitting clothes).[11]

In short, these rules formalised the need to keep a low profile, something everybody agreed on, which would lead to "acceptance", as indicated in the words concluding the rules: "Better acceptance by the community = improved security". It is worth noting that this notion of acceptance, introduced to MSF via security manuals,[12] was used extensively by members of the mission to describe a very wide range of practices and behaviours: no smoking in public, providing maternity care and meeting with local authorities.

In early March, just as work on refurbishing the hospital was about to begin, an incident occurred that made it seem that a project would have to be abandoned yet again. A delegation of Qabassin residents informed the project coordinator that they opposed the opening of a hospital because they feared that the town, so far unscathed, would become a target of bombardment by the regime. Remembering the failure of the prematurely opened Kafr Ghan project, the project coordinator took the time to understand and make sure of the project's backers and, during the period 9 to 16 March, he held numerous meetings. It transpired that the complaints were motivated as much by genuine fear as by frustrations stemming from the unequal distribution of the benefits prominent families stood to gain from MSF's project. So, after reassuring them, the refurbishment began and the recruitment process was initiated. The incident made the team more determined than ever to be as objective and transparent as possible, and they interviewed 300 candidates, from surgeons to cleaners. At the same time, the team took care to achieve a balance between Arabs and Kurds and between the various families for all posts not requiring any specific skills.

A Peaceful Little Town?

Networking I. (Establishing a Network of Contacts—How and Why)

After the hospital opened on 11 May 2013, the medical team concentrated on setting up activities. Although Qabassin remained calm, bombing and TNT barrel-bombs dropped from regime helicopters were daily occurrences across the Aleppo Governorate and there were sporadic rumours about the use of chemical weapons elsewhere in the country. It was this specific threat that led MSF's newly appointed (and very first) security focal point to make a visit to Syria in May 2013.

This was the background to the increasingly troubled relationship between the head of mission in Turkey and the new project coordinator, who had arrived in mid-April. The head of mission complained of "poor visibility" about the situation, which he blamed on inadequate communication on the part of the project coordinator.[13] He therefore asked him, starting with the tools and procedures, to show that he was paying sufficient attention to security matters. A morning and evening "security contact" was set up between the coordination team in Turkey and the project coordinator and initial hiccups further exacerbated tensions.[14] The head of mission accused the project coordinator of failing to use monitoring tools (the incidents database he had created and the board used to keep track of each team member's movements). Above all, he asked him to provide more detail about the context and to improve his network building. This included getting to know the people controlling checkpoints and obtaining their phone numbers, maintaining links with various groups and meeting newcomers, for, as well as Jabhat al-Nusra (the Al-Qaeda affiliate already present on the outskirts of Qabassin), other Salafist groups started setting up offices in June 2013. "You must communicate, build your network," the head of mission told him. In the Syrian context, where spy-fever was rife, and in the absence of anything specific to discuss, the project coordinator was firmly of the view that it was best to steer well clear:

"I felt it was necessary to stop asking people too many questions. (…) I'm convinced it was the right thing to do. Sometimes I feel it's inappropriate, the way we turn up and start questioning people (…).

And then there are the things that I know [being Muslim] about people who are a bit conservative, with radical tendencies. You're a guest; the fewer questions you ask, the greater your chances of being accepted."[15]

The same goes for the checkpoints: "Our laissez-passers worked everywhere; if they were letting us through, why ask questions?" He felt it more appropriate to observe and to "secure the relationship with our close entourage" of three or four regular contacts who had reassured him that "if the team toed the line, no one would harm us." Far from being settled by the change of head of mission in late June, the disagreement merely intensified, as his replacement was particularly focused on documenting the political and military context.

Disquiet (How to Interpret Information?)

While rumours of a major "battle for Aleppo" had been circulating since late May, June and July were in fact characterised by tensions and incidents within the opposition forces. These included clashes between PKK-affiliated Kurdish forces from Qabassin and police units acting under the authority of the Al-Bab Islamic court, the town falling under the provisional control of these Kurdish forces, and a bomb explosion at the Jabhat al-Nusra base just outside Qabassin. There were also confrontations at checkpoints between FSA brigades and fighters from a group newly arrived on the scene, known to be an offshoot of Al-Qaeda in Iraq and not on good terms with Jabhat al-Nusra: ISIS/ISIL or the Islamic State in Iraq and al-Sham/the Levant.[16]

At the end of July, the project coordinator reported back on these troubles, noting that, although Qabassin was currently "really quiet", Islamist groups (which included ISIS and Jabhat al-Nusra) further north in Jarabulus had announced their intention "of establishing an Islamic State" and had "declared that foreign NGOs are infidels and so not welcome in Syria." He added: "We've got all these groups in Qabassin."[17]

His mission ended on 30 July and, one week later, his replacement arrived (the project's third, including the set-up stage). From the start, he was alarmed by the situation he discovered, which contrasted strongly with the impression he had been given during his briefing back in Paris. As well as the heightened tensions between the various opposition groups, there had been two major incidents. The car bringing the project administrator back from the Turkish border to Qabassin after his leave had been held up by a group of armed men on the outskirts of the town. After apparently hesitating to kidnap the administrator, they had eventually left, taking with them the end-of-month wages he had been transporting. And, in Aleppo, an MSF-Spain car had been stopped by an armed group, and its occupants (a Syrian MSF logistician and two non-MSF passengers, said to be a Turkish contractor and his American girlfriend) were still being held prisoner.

By mid-August, the now very detailed emails the field team sent to the coordination team reported one concern after another. These included the team's lack of preparedness for a possible chemical attack, renewed ISIS statements attacking foreign NGOs in Jarabulus and rumours of a group targeting British citizens for kidnap, etc.[18] The project coordinator informed the coordination team that he wished to cut back the international staff immediately. The head of mission acquiesced, but not with the same urgency. 15 and 16 August saw clashes between Kurdish forces and the FSA/Islamist groups at various points across northern Syria. On 17 August, fighting broke out in Qabassin and that evening the project coordinator wrote to the head of mission: "everybody is safe at the house (...) ISIS now controls the town."[19]

An MSF Mission in "The Clutches of Islamic State of Iraq and al-Sham"

The first contact with ISIS took place at the MSF hospital when several combatants showed up after the fighting on 17 August. Two were injured and a third came complaining of stomach pains: "When we asked him to remove his coat, he said it was explosive and he couldn't take it off."[20]

The fighting had lasted just a day and calm was restored on 18 August. At the MSF house, the project coordinator and medical advisor interviewed each international staff member in turn. Were they willing to stay in an environment where "Al-Qaeda, in this case one of its affiliates, ISIS, is now fully in control of Qabassin?"[21] Nine of the fourteen team members chose to leave the mission and, by 19 August, they were all in Turkey.[22] The arrival of ISIS had enabled the project coordinator to get what he wanted and cut back the team in quite drastic fashion.

The five international staff who remained in Qabassin did not rule out following the others to Turkey. "What are we waiting for? For them to start executing our patients against the wall behind the hospital?" asked the nurse.[23] Predictions went back and forth between the coordination team and the team in the field. The project coordinator reported that a Syrian staff member said: "They want to establish an Islamic State [in Qabassin]." "That doesn't necessarily mean there's no place for MSF," replied the head of mission, "it depends on the degree of tolerance of the group as a whole as well as on their commander here." To which the project coordinator replied: "Can you give me one example of a place where they have sole power, where they have proclaimed the State, and where people like us are tolerated for very long?"[24] Based on his twenty-five years' experience with MSF (including eight years as president), the project coordinator was not optimistic. His research backed up his instinct: "I went online to look into their behaviour in recent years. In terms of civilian casualties, they're quite simply the most murderous of Al-Qaeda's branches," he wrote a few days later.[25]

Yet, on 19 August, the new ISIS representative in Qabassin paid the project coordinator a visit, assuring him that MSF could stay and work in safety. He agreed to put this commitment in writing:

In the name of Allah, the beneficent, the merciful,

Thanks be to Allah, peace and blessings be upon his prophet Mohammad.

From now on, the MSF hospital can continue treating all cases without bias to any party. MSF will consult the Islamic State in Qabassin if any problems arise at the hospital. And the Islamic State takes responsibility for protecting the hospital in the event of any danger. All doctors, men and women, can carry on working at the hospital.[26]

Networking II. (What Does "To Drink Tea" Signify?)

MSF also received unsolicited written support from important local contacts such as the local council and the Al-Bab Islamic court, whose various members were wary of ISIS's takeover of Qabassin. Right from the beginning of his mission, the project coordinator had met with as many people as he could and had even established cordial relations with some of them, such as a military judge at the Al-Bab court with links to the Ahrar al-Sham Islamist group, and a prominent citizen of Qabassin and member of the Free Syrian Army. Several would occasionally turn up unannounced at the house to talk. "I didn't really make any new contacts, but maybe I treated them differently," said the project coordinator. So when, for example, the local council or the Islamic court approached him to provide material assistance to displaced people, "I said 'ok, let's go and see what we can do', and that's how we came to spend a fair amount of time together." The project coordinator saw this as more about running the project than managing security. But time spent with local contacts did help to get a better grasp of the situation—the needs and the political currents—which he viewed as "the first stage in security." He and other members of the team would spend evenings and Friday afternoons in the company of these contacts and, in these more informal settings, "we didn't pretend to be neutral." They would chat and listen to the Syrians' accounts of "the early days of the revolution."

> According to Syrian social norms, when you pay somebody a visit you score a point. (...) If you answer an invitation you are honouring your host. It establishes a connection, a situation where it's ok for you to ask for something, or to be asked; it's a two-way thing—are you prepared to trade? If the answer's yes, then you need to establish relationships, while being aware of the social norms. (...) Sure, people ask you for favours, but then you ask for lots too! It worked both ways, and it's absolutely vital that it does.[27]

This is in very stark contrast to his predecessor:

> "I don't go to eat in people's homes. You need to be careful about accepting an invitation. Sometimes it's a two-way thing, and that's not a trap I want to fall into. So, I thank them for the invitation, no more than that, and we respect each other.

You need to keep your distance; I can drink tea with them in the office, chat at the hospital or in the street without having to visit their homes. And as we didn't know how the situation would play out... There's a saying in Arabic: "remember that we have shared salt at my home." (...) It related to my role as project coordinator. I wanted to maintain that distance that would allow me, if one day the need arose, to say: "I owe you nothing, and you owe me nothing."[28]

So, behind the consensual phrase "to drink tea" were two diametrically opposed practices.

Disagreements about the Situation Analysis

Despite reassurances obtained from local contacts and the Islamic State of Iraq and al-Sham, the project coordinator was still uneasy about the project's future. He felt that the fact that the coordination team and head office seemed fairly reassured simply meant they were failing to comprehend the extent of the danger. This was the case regarding the management of several human resource issues. Replacing the administrator was the subject of heated debate. As the only Muslim and Arab-speaker among the international staff, he was known in the small world of Qabassin and thus had a vital role in maintaining and gathering information. The coordination team wanted him to end his mission at the end of August as planned, to which the project coordinator answered that he was willing to stay on for longer and that his departure would seriously endanger the mission. Questions about the number and profiles of international staff led to yet more disagreement. While numbers had been increased to nine in order to resume surgical activities, Paris wanted to send in more international staff as well as visitors from head office. And lastly, an American doctor who arrived at the end of August let it slip that he was Jewish. He was asked to maintain absolute discretion about his origins; already in early August, even before ISIS arrived, the project coordinator had been forced to replace a Sri Lankan doctor who had created upset among staff and patients in the emergency room when he revealed that he was a Buddhist.[29]

Amid these preoccupations, on 21 August came the news that the regime had used chemical weapons in Damascus suburb Ghouta, a devastating manifestation of the threat that had been on people's minds for months. The team on the ground asked the coordination team to send in drugs to treat a possible flood of contaminated patients as well as to respond to requests made by very worried local council health officials. There was outrage when they were told that the drugs they already had—enough to treat a few dozen patients—would suffice for now. They also wanted to prepare for the admittedly quite unlikely possibility of chemical attack against Qabassin or Al-Bab. The protective gear (suit, mask, gloves, boots) was a real organisational headache as it was hard to use, bulky and expensive. So the organisation had made its choice: the team in Qabassin had a little more protective equipment than there were international members of staff. Several team members found this unspoken hierarchy in terms of protecting lives hard to swallow; what were they supposed to do about the national staff, their families and the patients?[30]

Adjustments (How to Justify MSF's Presence in Light of the Risks?)

"ISIS have asked us to continue to work with an international team in Qabassin. This is both dangerous and of little use,"[31] was the project coordinator's assessment in relation to what the project was delivering. He felt that the number of births was low (averaging ten per week) and that the hospital saw very few casualties, as most were treated at field hospitals set up by the various military groups (ISIS also had its own facility at a location unknown to MSF). The majority of procedures in the surgical unit were for burns (averaging twenty-four new cases per week), some very serious and which the project coordinator felt would be better treated in Turkey than in the MSF hospital. He therefore suggested "pulling out the international team from ISIS's clutches before things go really wrong", relocating the project to Al-Bab (where the opposition forces were more balanced, as reflected in the make-up of the Islamic court) and transferring responsibility for Qabassin to national staff.[32] "I didn't agree!" recalls MSF's president. As head of the emergency desk team when the Syria mission was being set up, he was still in contact with military commanders he had encountered in Atmah, one a Chechen jihadist who was a member of the *Muhajireen* (or 'exiles'), which went on to become a key element of ISIS. The jihadist reiterated that MSF was not in danger in Qabassin.[33] As for the head of mission, he argued that what had been achieved in Qabassin was not so bad, but authorised the project coordinator to further explore suggestions for adapting activities.

In the meantime, the team set out to redress the balance between the activities and the risks, by further developing activities. The doctor in charge of outreach, who had arrived at the beginning of August, was encouraged by the project coordinator to assess areas where displaced people had settled—they had already been visited by his predecessor but no action had been taken—such as As-Safirah to the south of Qabassin. In this constantly bombed area receiving no assistance whatsoever, small operations were set up to distribute medical supplies, tents and basic items, giving the team the sense of being "where we're needed."[34]

Procedures for travelling to As-Safirah consisted of making contact with Syrian contacts on site (a doctor and displaced persons manager) the day before, then getting an update on the actual day, notably via Twitter. If the decision was taken to travel, the MSF doctor met up with the two Syrians just outside the bombarded zone. "Stay close to the guy with the walkie-talkie. He gets real-time military information," the project coordinator instructed him.[35] The MSF doctor exposed himself to risks that he says he was "ultimately" not ready to take. He confided: "I set aside time every Friday to ask myself whether it was worth being there" and every week he answered in the affirmative. Paradoxically, by increasing the volume of activities and running operations that were riskier—but that the team felt to be more relevant—identified dangers became more acceptable.

The team's cohesion during that time undoubtedly contributed to the willingness to take risks: the project coordinator reported daily to his colleagues on the content of his meetings, sharing his interpretations and doubts. According to the medical advisor, this approach differed from that adopted by the previous project coordinator, for whom "nobody had the right to get involved in security issues because that was the project coordinator's role." "It felt a bit like he didn't want to talk about security because he didn't want to worry people: 'let me worry about security, and you worry about medical stuff.'" However—and this comes up time and again in interviews—it was by becoming better informed about the significant danger around them that the team found themselves more "at ease". The risks were appraised and carefully considered, and they were able to witness the efforts that went into minimising them as much as it was possible. Presumably, they also appreciated knowing what they were exposing themselves to so that they could decide for themselves whether the risks were worth taking.

Another factor was that the team's day-to-day routine had not been impacted by the town falling to ISIS. The fighters were keeping a low profile, leaving Qabassin's local council and Islamic court to manage day-to-day affairs. Apart from the destruction of a Sufi saint's tomb, ISIS had not taken any hostile action or introduced any radical measures contrary to local practices. Female international staff already wore long dresses and headscarves, so did not have to alter their clothing. By the end of August, the project coordinator, who had banned going out on foot immediately after the fall of Qabassin, felt it was time to put a stop to the "bunker syndrome" and encouraged international staff to get out and interact with people.[36] Mindful of his previous experience with Islamist groups, he nonetheless took the view that the "honeymoon" between ISIS and MSF would be short-lived. After the group's initial attempt at winning over local people, which would include respect for MSF, a "deterioration"[37] in the relationship would follow. But how could the exact moment when it would become too dangerous be anticipated?

From One Guarantee to the Next: Incidents, Negotiations and Breakdown

Red Lines (What Constitutes a Serious Incident?)

On 2 September, a Syrian surgeon from MSF-Spain's Bab al-Salama project was kidnapped in the middle of the night from the house occupied by Syrian staff. He was tortured and murdered. No group claimed responsibility, but for MSF-Spain there was no doubting that the act was in response to the doctor's openly atheist views.[38] The Spanish section concluded that this was a personal affair and did not target the association "as such."[39] The kidnap-murder caused significant tension between the various MSF sections. For once in agreement, MSF staff in Qabassin, Reyhanli and Paris were angered that, as in Aleppo a few weeks before when its car had been stopped and its passengers abducted, the Spanish section seemed reluctant to share its information—or at least its suspicions about who was responsible. Furthermore, the Bab al-Salama team had been evacuated without informing MSF's other projects, indicating in the view of the Qabassin project coordinator "a total lack of consideration for teams on the ground who need information if they are to stay safe."[40]

On 19 September, ISIS captured Azaz, bringing MSF-Spain's Bab al-Salama project under its control.[41] Then, on 25 September, teams on the ground learned that the previous seven days had seen much chatter on social media in response to a tweet on 18 September by an ISIS member showing a photo of an international MSF worker and stating: "#ISIS publishes a map of bases used by missionary spy doctors working for MSF." The MSF members who had passed on the information advised against responding. "It's easy to decide not to respond when you're not the one at risk," commented the exasperated project coordinator, who proposed to counter-campaign on social networks by publishing letters of support from ISIS to MSF.[42] His mission ended a few days later.

After a gap of ten days, a new project coordinator arrived on 12 October for just one month. The next day, a serious incident occurred in the hospital's surgical unit when several casualties were brought to the hospital after an altercation with men from the Al-Bab Islamic court who had come to arrest them. Three of the patients were taken away to be judged, two of whom died a few days later from lack of proper treatment. The third was executed by shooting and, on 18 October, the men from the Islamic court brought his body back to the MSF hospital.

Then began a dialogue of the deaf between the project coordinator and the coordination team on the significance of the incident and how MSF should react. As the project coordinator saw it, the men from the Islamic court, who had not been aggressive, "simply did what they had to do to fulfil their objective." "None of us are comfortable with it, but we're aware that we couldn't have done much about it," he added. At least "the worst was avoided, meaning shooting inside or around the hospital." The next step was to meet "the Al-Bab and Qabassin courts to talk about what would happen if suspects were taken to the hospital in the future" and "regularly remind all the groups encountered of the principle of no-weapons in the hospital."[43] The head of mission[44] felt that the project coordinator's reaction was unsatisfactory and was worried about his attempts to calm things down.[45] On 22 October, the operations department in Paris got involved, insisting that inflicting physical harm on patients should be considered as a "red line" that called for MSF to express its indignation and ask the authorities to renew their guarantees. The project coordinator was asked to go back to see his contacts and "lay the cards on the table."[46]

At the same time, the rest of the team appeared somewhat unconcerned. The now many international staff members (back up to around fifteen), almost all newly arrived, were kept in the dark about the discussions between the project coordinator and the coordination team. Present since August, the outreach doctor was the only one to still feel very uneasy.[47] They were thus all somewhat bewildered (and the doctor relieved) when, following notification from the French Ministry of Foreign Affairs of a threat to "kidnap two MSF doctors", the coordination team requested an immediate reduction in staff numbers (the outreach doctor was among those who left). Travel restrictions were imposed and French staff still present were advised to leave soon. It was also decided not to post any more French citizens to Qabassin, as was already the case for US citizens.

Following this sudden revelation of the dangers around them, as of 4 November, the team became gripped by anxiety. That day, three ISIS fighters turned up at MSF and requisitioned an ambulance, promising to return it in four or five days. The medical advisor recalled that it was at that moment she realised she risked being kidnapped. "I said to myself: 'today they're taking the vehicle; tonight they might come to the house and take me.'"[48]

(Re)negotiate, But How Far Should We Go?

Following these incidents, the president of MSF-France travelled to Syria. He and the new head of mission (the fourth since the start of the project who arrived in early November) made a visit to Qabassin to try and meet with representatives of ISIS from Qabassin and Al-Bab. The Al-Bab representative, "a Sudanese man everybody was terrified of", received them and provided the guarantees they sought regarding MSF's presence and its international staff—including French citizens. The Qabassin representative agreed to appoint a civilian intermediary who would from then on convey any ISIS demands. On the journey back, the president met with his Chechen contact from Atmah and asked him to confirm the validity of these assurances, "He said: 'stop worrying! I'm telling you that you can do your work.'"[49]

Buoyed by these reassurances, the new head of mission felt it possible to handle ISIS' demands more calmly. Making the odd donation of medicines or small items of equipment was, in his view, the price to pay for maintaining a dialogue with the group, which had to be acknowledged as the de facto authority. This attitude was in contrast to that of his predecessor (who considered unacceptable any donations to the "armed group")[50] as well as of the new project coordinator, who was sceptical about whether it was possible to work with ISIS.[51] These differences of opinion became yet more patent after a second MSF ambulance was commandeered on December 18, as one saw a red line, and the other sought to play it down. "We don't pack our bags over an ambulance (...); for an ambulance you renegotiate." Three days later the vehicle was returned, fitted with new tyres, and the debate rolled on: stay, yes, but until when, just how far should we go? The logistics coordinator summed up MSF's implicit response to this question:

> I think only under extreme circumstances will the organisation decide to cease activities, for example, if an international employee is kidnapped or attacked. For most other incidents, it's a question of negotiating with everyone involved to decide HOW we can continue our activities, not IF we continue our activities.[52]

Kidnap

On 2 January in Bernas, Idlib province, five international staff from the MSF-Belgium project were kidnapped by ISIS, then under great pressure from other Islamist groups and FSA brigades which went on to launch a major offensive against it the following day. On 4 January, a trusted source told the Qabassin project coordinator that the same armed groups had decided to rid the town of ISIS. He advised MSF to keep out of harm's way for a while and, the next day, all international personnel were in Turkey.

MSF-Belgium asked all sections to maintain their activities in Syria as long as the negotiations to free the hostages lasted. The Qabassin project continued to operate with Syrian staff alone and remote supervision by a project coordinator based in Turkey. Incidents such as arrests and intimidation involving national staff increased and some left the town. The period of winning over the civilian population was well and truly over.

The hostages were freed after five months of captivity in the spring of 2014. In Qabassin, ISIS representatives asked MSF to return, arguing that they were being penalised for the behaviour of their counterparts in Bernas. But in view of the loss of trust caused by the kidnap itself, the treatment meted out to the hostages and the demands made for their release, MSF called for explanations and further guarantees from the very highest levels of the organisation. Several letters were addressed to the "inner circle"; none received an answer. On 21 August 2014, MSF officially announced the cessation of all its activities in Islamic State-controlled territory.

Pictures of the execution of American journalist James Foley had been released two days previously. Four Western hostages, three of them aid workers, would be beheaded before the end of the year. On 6 February 2015, the Islamic State announced the death of Kayla Mueller, a young aid worker who, it transpired, was the woman kidnapped in the MSF-Spain vehicle in August 2013.

* * *

It is very difficult to look at the history of the Qabassin mission without being influenced by what we now know about how events played out for MSF and, more importantly, about Islamic State. While its very name today inspires dread, this group was little-known in August 2013, and those best informed at MSF viewed it as a sort of "Al-Qaeda, Mark 2." Until it captured Qabassin, the teams (rightly) saw clashes between armed groups, and most of all bombing by the regime, as the most serious risks to themselves. As for kidnappings, journalists had been abducted from 2012 on and the threat was viewed with varying degrees of gravity depending on the successive heads of mission—but in Qabassin in 2013 this threat was consistently perceived as remote given how well-accepted the project was. This perception did not alter until the arrival of the project coordinator in charge during August and September, which was closely followed by that of ISIS. These factors underline the difficulty of what is known in humanitarian aid jargon as "context analysis" (forming the basis for risk analysis)—rather like trying to feel the way forward in thick fog by identifying, singling out and analysing scraps of contradictory, and sometimes confused, information. This task is still more arduous when information is lost due to a rapid succession of project coordinators, usually with no handover period, not to mention the gaps during which the post is held by a replacement for a few days or even left vacant.

In this regard, analysis of the Qabassin project appears to show that practices intended to compile as much intelligence as possible in order to obtain exhaustive information—be it via a multiplication of tracking tools, incident reports and statistical data, or compiling politico-military events, press dispatches and articles—do not always help when it comes to analysing a context. While they have their uses, they also take up much time and energy because of their non-selective nature. It may also be assumed that the coordinators would have learnt of the most pertinent facts among all this information sought so vigorously, provided their network of contacts had been working effectively. The story of the Qabassin project shows time and again the importance of quality relationships, something that the expression "to drink tea" does not, as we have demonstrated, necessarily describe with its masking of opposing practices. Several members of the project team maintained such relationships with their Syrian colleagues and contacts external to the organisation, which helped them not only to gain an understanding of the local dynamics but also ensured a constant flow of information. It also enabled a sharing of crucial information that afforded the team at least a few hours' notice of what was going to happen, such as when the team was evacuated in January 2014. Contrary to the usual recommendations, trust in these instances was not built so much on invoking "MSF principles", adopting a neutral stance and a "standard" discourse, as on relationship-building, dialogue, careful listening, a kind of openness—necessarily combined with respect for the codes and beliefs held by others—and "dependability": "do what we said we would do and say what we did."[53]

Nevertheless, the end of the story also serves to highlight the limitations of the guarantees derived from some of these relationships. We have placed much emphasis on differences in analyses made by, on the one hand, those in the field, and on the other, the coordination team and head office in the immediate aftermath of ISIS' takeover, as well as on the differing degrees of disquiet of the successive project coordinators and heads of mission (a disquiet felt far more in the field than at head office). Leaving aside the subtleties and nuances in the various points of view, these divergences related to whether assurances from ISIS representatives were to be trusted. The consistently affirmative response provided by head office to this question, in the face of the concerns expressed by those in the field, was directly linked to the assurances MSF's president obtained through the close relationship he had established with several important contacts who had proved to be trustworthy since the opening of the Atmah project. Conversely, it was because he judged ISIS to be different to all the other armed groups operating in northern Syria that the project coordinator on site during August and September was pessimistic and gave these assurances little credibility. His pessimism was rooted in his experience with jihadi groups, in what he had heard from national staff and other contacts in Qabassin and Al-Bab, and also in his personal research into the group, its statements, writings and publications, its political programme—in short, its ideology.

But what this story also shows is that, despite everything, MSF stayed. Regular challenging of the relevance of the project, the deterioration predicted by some, Twitter accusations of spying, rumours about the kidnap threat from France's Ministry of Foreign Affairs, the incidents in October and December, the murder of the Syrian doctor and the kidnap of MSF-Belgium's five international staff—none of these led the team to pull out. Evacuation (supposedly temporary) was finally ordered on the basis of detailed information provided by a reliable source on an imminent outbreak of hostilities. Once the team left, senior managers realised they were "relieved."[54] The fact that successive teams were kept in place provides much food for thought about the way in which MSF functions as an institution as well as the reasons that motivate individuals to stay in a situation and accept substantial risks. These reasons may be rooted in an attachment to a place, to their work, a refusal to abandon a civilian population, or to less easily avowed sentiments, such as the thrill felt at certain moments or not wanting to let down MSF by a failure to overcome fear.

8

THE SHADOWY THEATRE OF KIDNAPPINGS

AN ACCOUNT OF ARJAN ERKEL'S RESCUE

Duncan McLean

"In spite of the broad solidarity that individual persons and international organizations demonstrated towards Arjan Erkel, today, it must be underlined that the management of his case remains a failure:

Failure of the Russian authorities that have legal responsibility to solve the case. Failure of the Dutch Government who have maintained a low profile diplomatic approach to the case. Failure of partner governments of the Russian Federation that remained largely passive and indulgent, allowing the escalation of violence towards humanitarians in the region. And failure of MSF for trusting that all of the above were doing their utmost to resolve the case and would do so automatically without requiring mounting public pressure to be applied by MSF."

Médecins Sans Frontières, "Arjan Erkel, Hostage in the Russian Federation since August 12, 2002: One Year of a Kidnapping", press pack prepared for the briefing on the occasion of the one-year anniversary of Arjan Erkel's abduction in August 2003.

Arjan Erkel, MSF-Switzerland's head of mission in Dagestan, was kidnapped in the suburbs of regional capital Makhachkala on 12 August 2002 and freed in somewhat obscure circumstances 607 days later. Arjan's captivity was punc-

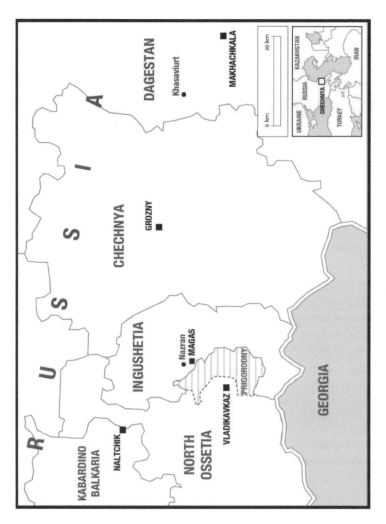

Map 4: Russian Caucasus

tuated by episodes of considerable publicity, many initiated by MSF, with some, like the example above, epitomising the frequent conflicts opposing the Erkel family, the Dutch government and MSF, despite all three parties sharing the same stated objective of securing his release.

The entire affair is unusual, both in the lengthy court case that opposed the Dutch government and MSF and in the many accounts of his abduction that have been published.[1] In conjunction with interviews of the principal actors and internal reports, these documents provide a rare window of analysis into the experience and dilemmas faced by an aid organisation seeking to obtain the release of one of its employees.

Missing

MSF in the Caucasus

Right from their first interventions in the Caucasus in the early 1990s, and more particularly in Chechnya, MSF teams were confronted with a context of denial of access, intimidation and extreme violence. The First Chechen War (1994–1996) resulted in the near decimation of its population[2], while the Second (1999–2009) saw the military occupation of the country by 100,000 Russian Federation troops from April 2002 onward. Occurring on a daily basis, insurgent attacks and counter-insurgency operations created a climate of terror. According to human rights organisations, at least 25,000 civilians disappeared or lost their lives between 1999 and 2007.[3]

During both Chechen Wars, MSF was outspoken in drawing attention to the tremendous human cost of these conflicts as well as the danger of delivering aid.[4] This was tragically illustrated on 17 December 1996 with the murder of six delegates of the International Committee of the Red Cross (ICRC) in their field hospital in Novye Atagi. MSF was no stranger to the perils of the region as a total of sixteen of its employees were detained or kidnapped in the Caucasus between 1993 and 2004.[5]

A long-standing tradition in the region, hostage-taking took on an entirely new dimension during the First Chechen War. Arbitrary arrests and detentions of Chechens by Russian and pro-Russian forces led to the practice of exchanging or selling live and dead prisoners. This use of prisoners as bargaining chips was the prelude to the wave of kidnappings that was to sweep through the North Caucasus after the first war.[6] Involving all segments of society—gangs, clans, rebels, security forces, politicians, entrepreneurs, etc.—the flourishing human trafficking industry targeted local residents, Russians and foreigners alike, as illustrated (among others) by the abduction on 19 January 1998 of the head of UNHCR's North Ossetia office, Vincent Cochetel (freed 317 days later),[7] and the kidnap of International Red Cross nurse Geraldo Cruz on 16 May 1999 in Kabardino–Balkaria (released in late July).[8]

Prior to Arjan's abduction, the latest MSF member to be kidnapped had been Kenny Gluck, head of mission for the Dutch section. Abducted in January 2001, he was held in Chechnya for twenty-six days before being unconditionally released. Unlike most previous cases, which had involved the Chechen mafia and networks with Russian connections, Kenny had been kidnapped by an Islamist Chechen resistance group. He was released with a "letter of apology", signed by its leader Shamil Basayev himself. Later posted on pro-independent Chechen website Kavkaz.org the letter explained that Kenny had been kidnapped by a group of mujahideen hoping to negotiate his release in exchange for comrades and family members abducted by Russian military forces. It stated that a High Sharia Court had decided to release him unconditionally because of his humanitarian work. "We also inform you that when examining your case, the Assembly of the High Sharia Court decided to forbid the abductions of members of humanitarian agencies," the letter concluded.[9]

The benevolence shown by the Chechen opposition towards Kenny Gluck did not improve the already strained relations between Moscow and MSF, regularly accused in the pro-government press of siding with the separatists.[10] Tensions were further heightened by disagreements over the planned tripartite agreement between Russia, Chechnya and neighbouring Russian republic Ingushetia to repatriate some 200,000 internally displaced persons (IDPs) to Chechnya. MSF voiced concerns over the forced return of civilians to a war zone at a time when Chechnya was subject to *zatchiski*, i.e. "clean-up" operations executed by masked men travelling around in armoured vehicles with unidentifiable plates whose job it was to torture and slaughter civilians suspected of supporting the insurgents.[11]

By mid-2002, MSF operations in Chechnya, Ingushetia and Dagestan included running mobile clinics, supporting hospitals and dispensaries (through the provision of medical supplies and rehabilitation of essential services) as well as assisting displaced populations. The fear of kidnap and targeted attacks against aid agencies had led MSF, in the spring of 2002, to significantly reduce its international staff in the Caucasus.

Unlike Chechnya, neighbouring Dagestan had not plunged into civil war. However, at the turn of the new millennium, it was the second poorest republic in the Russian Federation and the fringes of the Chechen War created an opportunity for gangsters, politicians and businessmen looking to make a profit, notably through arms and human trafficking. Shackled to Moscow, which provided 90 per cent of the Republic's state budget, Dagestan was prey to rampant corruption, as illustrated by the nebulous role played by "police officers [working] for the state, their clan and their crime organisation simultaneously."[12]

MSF was relatively new to Dagestan. In March 2000, the Swiss section had conducted an exploratory mission with the objective of gaining access to Chechnya and setting up a small operation in Dagestan itself. Despite various warnings, particularly from the press,[13] the section had concluded that Dagestan was, for the time being, relatively safe. Small-scale activities limited to rehabilitation and vaccination programmes were set up along with distributions of non-food items for displaced Chechens.

The Abduction

His predecessors having alternated every few months, Arjan Erkel was the Swiss section's first permanent head of mission in Dagestan. He arrived in mid-April 2002 as the region's humanitarian agenda was dominated by the tripartite plan to repatriate IDPs to Chechnya. Arjan attended internal MSF meetings in Paris during which strategies were outlined to lobby and advocate publicly against the forced return of displaced Chechens.

In mid-July, the Office of the United Nations' Security Coordinator informed MSF that the FSB (Federal Security Service of the Russian Federation, ex-KGB) had given warning of an increased risk of abduction. It was assumed by the various MSF sections that the warning was a measure of intimidation to reduce the presence of NGOs and curb their campaigning against the repatriation plan. However, after Nina Davydovich, head of Russian NGO Druzhba, was abducted in Chechnya on 23 July, there was general agreement within MSF to evacuate those international personnel still present and freeze national staff travel in the Caucasus.[14]

The Swiss section still considered Dagestan safe and made an exception for the area, where it continued its operations. During the same period, Arjan was contacted by a US Embassy military attaché requesting security information and logistical assistance with a visit to Dagestan. On his own initiative, on 4 August, Arjan sent a car to Makhachkala airport to pick up the officer and another American attaché and later dined with them. No other MSF staff were present at the dinner. Indeed, all those consulted opposed contact with the Americans due not only to the incompatibility of their and MSF's missions, but also to the skewed perceptions this could provoke.[15]

It was not until a second FSB warning was received on 6 August—this time relayed directly to the Swiss section via their Khasavyurt office—that international staff were reduced and restricted to Makhachkala. Arjan remained and pursued a number of discussions with Dagestan security agencies, who provided reassurances that there was no increased risk to MSF's teams. Nevertheless, the analysis of his Dutch counterpart in Moscow, relayed by Arjan to the head office in Geneva, would echo previous FSB warnings: "MSF-Holland thinks it will not be quiet until a big fish is kidnapped."[16]

Shortly after, on 12 August, Arjan was snatched from outside his girlfriend's home in the suburbs of Makhachkala. Although slightly injured during the abduction, by his own account he was subsequently treated relatively well. He was held for a week by his kidnappers and then passed on to "keepers" operating on behalf of unseen "owners". Over the course of the next twenty months, Arjan would be detained at various locations. He was never permitted to see the faces of his captors but nonetheless built a rapport of sorts with them. Bits and pieces of information would filter through to him, partly reflecting possible avenues for his liberation but more often than not false hopes.[17]

The Wait (August–December 2002)

The Initial Reactions of MSF, Arjan's Family and the Dutch Government

Launching a crisis plan based on MSF-Holland's standard protocol, the morning after the kidnapping MSF-Switzerland set up a crisis cell in Geneva under the responsibility of the Dagestan programme manager. The cell was later reinforced with internal specialists in human resources, communications, context analysis and administration. During the following month, field crisis cells were sent to Moscow and Makhachkala with support from other sections, primarily MSF-France. Overall supervision fell to a steering committee made up of MSF-Switzerland's president, director general and director of operations.[18]

While day-to-day operations and decisions remained with the Swiss section, the Dutch section was involved from the start. Initially, their participation consisted of the Dutch head of mission (MSF's only head of mission in the country at the time) assuming temporary responsibility for the crisis cell in Moscow until reinforcements could be sent in from Geneva. In addition, in view of Arjan's nationality, a crisis cell was also established in Amsterdam. The primary role of this cell was to provide support with dealing with the Dutch Foreign Ministry and managing relations with the Erkel family "with a bit more cultural sensitivity."[19]

Informed on the day of the abduction, the family were far from self-effacing. To draw the attention of Dutch government circles to Arjan's plight, his father Dick Erkel immediately started lobbying Dutch Foreign Affairs officials. A member of the ruling CDA[20] party, Erkel's political connections enabled him to meet with the Dutch Foreign Minister in person within the first few weeks of the kidnapping and, more generally, to access government officials.[21]

To begin with, the Dutch Foreign Ministry treated the kidnapping as a simple consular affair, but the case came to be afforded more importance with the involvement of senior officials within the administration. This included the setting up of a crisis cell headed by the director for consular affairs and frequent interventions by his superiors, but did not alter a policy of "silent diplomacy" whereby the Dutch government would officially limit its role to that of a facilitator and nothing more.[22] The Hague was formally committed to a policy of non-payment of ransoms and non-negotiation with hostage-takers, but did not prevent families, employers or other benefactors from doing so in their stead. The Dutch government seemed all the more reluctant to become directly involved as Russia was a key strategic and economic partner. Indeed, in 2003, Moscow had become the main supplier of crude oil to the Netherlands, and the country ranked as the Russian Federation's third trading and investment partner.[23]

The Silence of the Kidnappers

Shortly after the abduction, rumours circulated in the local press as to who was responsible—the FSB, bandits or Chechen rebels. Claiming to know who the culprits were, Dagestani leaders blamed "Wahhabis, radical Muslims, the enemies of Russia", while insinuating that the abduction was intended to demonstrate that Dagestan was still "dangerous and unstable."[24] Meanwhile, a number of humanitarian agencies made the connection between the kidnappings of Arjan Erkel and Nina Davydovich and the plan to repatriate Chechen refugees from Ingushetia. As one journalist reported in August 2002: "Under cover of anonymity, the heads of humanitarian organisations in Moscow stated yesterday that the purpose of these kidnappings was to make NGOs leave Chechnya and the surrounding republics as the refugees begin returning home."[25]

In accordance with the usual recommendations drawn up by specialists in kidnap management, the MSF-Switzerland crisis cell initially adopted a patient, low-key approach.[26] Hoping that the Russian or rebel leaders would resolve the case quickly, the cell decided to "minimis[e] interferences and wait for the phone call" from the kidnappers, an intermediary or the authorities. During meetings behind closed doors, MSF appealed to Russian and Dagestani officials to provide "any information or any contact that may lead to a solution of the problem" while promising to "keep strict confidentiality on any support we obtain."[27] Discretion was used in other initiatives, such as activating local networks and establishing contacts—including among Chechen opposition groups. The Dutch, French and Belgian sections were solicited for help with expanding these networks and attempts were made to consult with journalists, scholars and regional experts, particularly by the MSF team in Moscow. Publically, the demand was for Arjan Erkel's "unconditional release", with MSF restricting its press releases to highlighting the "risks civilians and relief workers" were facing in the Caucasus.[28] Approved by Arjan's family, this approach fitted neatly with the Dutch government's preference for quiet diplomacy.

The October 2002 Nord-Ost theatre hostage crisis in Moscow was emblematic of the discretion maintained by MSF during the first months following Arjan's abduction. Despite being asked by the Chechen separatist hostage-takers to mediate, MSF kept a low operational and media profile, eventually providing medical supplies to local hospitals that had admitted survivors of the Russian Special Forces' assault on the theatre. The crisis ended in the death of 129 hostages out of 850, all but one killed by the combat gas used by the special forces during their assault. The FSB refused to disclose the chemical composition of the gas, which triggered outrage among Muscovite health workers who had been exposed to it while trying to resuscitate unconscious patients.[29] MSF made a conscious effort to stay discreetly in the background so as not to antagonise the Russian authorities and complicate attempts to obtain their help to get Arjan freed. Up to this point, MSF's communication on the kidnapping can be summarised as "saying next to nothing."[30]

A Change in Strategy (November 2002–August 2003)

Public Advocacy Makes a First Appearance
(November 2002–February 2003)

For the remainder of 2002, there were no attempts by those responsible for Arjan's abduction to contact MSF, the Dutch government or his family. The absence of a ransom demand or proof of life fuelled suspicions within MSF of broader political machinations behind the abduction.[31] As the then director of operations of MSF-Switzerland later recalled, "there was still this idea in the back of my mind that this type of exaction had to be authorized somewhere, that in this game, it's the people with the power who hold the cards."[32]

There was general agreement with the Dutch government that the Dagestani police and Russian authorities were doing little to resolve the case. Then, following the Nord-Ost crisis, the first high-level meeting attended by MSF representatives and FSB officials was held. According to the MSF delegation, the FSB passed on a message that could not have been more clear. Arjan's abduction "was the kind of thing that happened to people who pissed them off, people like us".[33]

Within MSF, the low-key approach adopted by the Geneva crisis cell was starting to be called into question. Opinions diverged on how best to push the Russian authorities into finding a resolution. Continue with silent diplomacy or publicly embarrass the Kremlin? An earlier move by MSF-Holland to contract a private security consultancy firm, Control Risks Group, had also triggered internal controversy.[34] Intended to reassure the family that "we would not put our principles above the utility of saving a life," the move was poorly received by not only the crisis cell but also the French section. They criticised the lack of added value that such a group could provide and the damaging impact on MSF's image of contracting a private security company known for its ambiguous links with Western secret services while Arjan's meeting with US military attachés had already raised suspicions about MSF's links to such services.[35]

By the end of 2002, the lack of progress in securing Arjan's release convinced MSF-Switzerland's director of operations to set up a brainstorming group to look into options not currently explored by the crisis cell and enable differences of opinion to be aired.[36] This "advisory group" comprised of key figures from the MSF International Office and the French, Dutch, US and Swiss sections, was not intended to replace the decision-making Geneva crisis cell and steering committee. It was during its first meeting in mid-November that the group suggested using the media to apply political pressure, first on the Russian authorities, and then the Dutch.

As the subsequent Geneva crisis cell communication plan would confirm, in an attempt to draw attention to the case (in private and then publicly), it was now time to step up the pressure on the Russian authorities to get them to secure Arjan's release by underlining their legal responsibility to do so.[37] Initially, this would involve targeted lobbying of key international actors such as the UN, the US, Russia and the Chechen opposition, and, depending on the results of this lobbying, a public communication campaign with a potentially "aggressive or denunciatory message."[38] It was later decided to tie in

Arjan's kidnapping with the broader political context, that is, a policy designed to deprive the Chechen population of humanitarian aid, with the passive consent of the international community.

The first obvious manifestation of the shift in MSF's tactic became clear in February 2003 as the crisis cell in Geneva announced its intention to hold a press conference in the presence of Dick Erkel and the Dutch ambassador in Moscow. The launch of a petition was to follow in March. Both the Dutch Foreign Ministry and the Erkel family voiced their concerns when they found out about the content of the new communication plan. The Ministry considered "direct accusations against the Russian authorities" problematic in securing their cooperation while the family felt an accusatory tone "could work against the case"[39]—a criticism they would renew several times in the months to come. Exposed to pressure from Dutch public opinion and "dominated by the family and the government,"[40] MSF-Holland would use the same arguments to question the relevance of the advocacy campaign.

The press conference went ahead on 12 February 2003, although MSF did tone down its rhetoric. In calling on the Russian and Dagestani authorities to secure Arjan's release, it was simply noted that the "non-resolution of this kidnapping may have a political dimension" and journalists were left to deduce the implications.[41] Less than a month later, an international petition demanding Arjan's release was launched, as the authorities "are not showing the slightest willingness to resolve this matter."[42] In the Dutch press, MSF-Holland's head of mission went even further, openly mooting a scenario of official Russian involvement: "It is possible that Arjan has been kidnapped by the security services or by someone else and that the authorities are happy to let it happen."[43] Yet meanwhile, during private meetings with Russian representatives, MSF was passing on the message that it was ready to drop its campaign, pay a "service fee" to facilitate Arjan's release, and offer public thanks to the Russian authorities for their efforts as soon as Arjan was freed.

In the meantime, information continued to emerge that pointed to the involvement of the Russian government in Arjan's kidnapping and/or its failure to be resolved. In March 2003, Arjan's mobile phone bill showed some sixty-one calls made after his abduction to various numbers in Moscow, the Caucasus and Rostov, including to policemen, members of the FSB, and known kidnapping intermediaries. Eventually dismissed by the Russian authorities as not relevant to the investigation, the number was disconnected shortly afterwards.[44] Then, in April 2003, the Moscow crisis team was informed by the Russian Federation's deputy prosecutor that the FSB had witnessed Arjan's abduction as they had been tailing him. The FSB justified their lack of assistance by claiming their agents were unarmed.[45] There was little doubt among MSF's decision-makers: if the kidnappers' identity and motives could not be established, at the very least, active obstruction on the part of the Russians was a fact.

First Proofs of Life (March–May 2003)

On 30 March 2003, while Arjan's father and brother were in Moscow for the handing over of the international petition to the Russian authorities, the Dutch government asked them to return immediately to The Hague. As soon as they got back, they and members of the MSF crisis cell were shown the first proof of life, allegedly secured by the "services of a third country". These were letters dating from late January, one addressed to each party. Accompanying the letters were photographs of Arjan. In the first he seemed relatively healthy, but in the second, taken on 27 February, he was unshaven and looked exhausted.

From MSF's perspective, the timing of the first proof of life, unquestionably a positive advance after seven and a half months of silence from the kidnappers, could be interpreted as confirming the relevance of the shift in communication strategy, epitomised by the press conference and press releases denouncing the Russian and Dagestani authorities' lack of willingness to resolve the case. More disturbingly, this proof of life was received right before more press conferences which the Russian and Dutch governments were particularly unhappy about.[46]

After the proof of life, there was a pause[47] in the media campaign as potential channels of negotiation with the kidnappers opened and then closed. MSF did not pursue a Dutch government "secret contact" in Baku (Azerbaijan) very seriously because of concerns about the security of the MSF envoy. Then, a South Caucasian intermediary in contact with the crisis cell had one of his own men kidnapped while he was trying to liaise with the kidnappers in Dagestan.

First Cycle of Negotiations Ends in Failure (May–September 2003)

In May 2003, MSF learned that the investigation into the kidnapping had been suspended by the Dagestani police as early as November 2002 and had only recently been reopened.[48] One month later, the FSB handed over a video of Arjan to the Dutch Embassy. It included a threat: Arjan would be killed if a ransom were not paid.

This reinforced the view within MSF that the Russian authorities could, should they want to, provide a resolution. This was seemingly confirmed when, in July, the FSB identified an intermediary of the kidnappers who was prepared to meet with MSF. During a meeting in Makhachkala, this intermediary passed on a demand for a ransom of US$5 million to the Dutch government and MSF's representatives (accompanied by an FSB-appointed "coach"), who requested proof of life before allowing the discussions to go any further.

A proof of life was delivered on 30 July, and Arjan later confirmed that around that time he was told to prepare for his release. Yet there was considerable frustration on the part of MSF that "if the FSB [was] capable of pulling strings behind the curtains", why could they not conduct the negotiations themselves?[49] On 12 August 2003, MSF launched its most forceful communication campaign to date to mark the one-year anniversary of Arjan's abduction. It denounced not only the Russian government, which must be "reminded of their legal responsibility", but also the "reserved attitude" of their Dutch counterparts.[50]

At this point, the communication channel opened up in Makhachkala via the intermediary identified by the FSB failed. Within the Swiss section, this failure was interpreted in very different ways. While the Geneva crisis cell concluded that this channel had already been blown, the head of the crisis cell in Moscow blamed the anniversary communication campaign. According to him, rather than a greater involvement of the Russian authorities in the negotiations, it had resulted in the FSB being unreceptive to the planned follow-up meeting. The Dutch Ambassador was furious for the same reason.[51]

Less than a month later, in September 2003, a potential deal set up through the auspices of a Dutch lawyer and intermediaries in Ingushetia (who had connections with organised crime) appeared sufficiently promising for MSF to authorise for safekeeping the transfer of €250,000 via the Dutch Foreign Ministry to its embassy in Moscow. According to the lawyer's intermediaries, the deal collapsed because of a police crackdown following the bombing on 15 September of the FSB headquarters in Ingushetia capital Magas. Further compounding the frustration was the Dagestani Ministry of the Interior's announcement—then retraction—that Arjan was alive.

The Path to Release (September 2003–April 2004)

The Press and FSB Veterans Join the Investigation
(September–December 2003)

By the end of 2003, the abduction and many of the details were being covered more extensively in the local and international media, irrespective of MSF's communication initiatives. Local and foreign journalists were also conducting their own investigations. Writing in *The New York Times* about the shutting down of the investigation in November 2002, Bob Herbert noted that it would have remained so, had MSF "not succeeded in turning the case into an embarrassment for the Putin government."[52] A number of articles by Coen van Zwol and by Vyacheslav Ismailov (the latter a *Novaya Gazeta* journalist and former Russian army officer) published various names of people who they alleged either had direct links to Arjan's kidnapping or had acted as intermediaries. Ismailov's investigations placed responsibility with a Dagestan Duma politician who was allegedly implicated in the April 2002 FSB assassination of a Saudi militant fighting alongside Chechen rebels. According to the journalist, the kidnapper was a "gangster boss that poses as a strict Muslim, but is a double agent of the FSB". As the kidnapper was also being sought by units of the Dagestani police, "Arjan Erkel [was] like a life insurance to him. 'If you will kill me, then you will kill Erkel and that means a loss of face for the FSB.' He plays around with this", stated Ismailov.[53]

By autumn 2003, another FSB-supported intermediary, a veterans' association of ex-security service personnel calling itself "Truth and Honour", provided a new opening that looked promising. Referred by Arjan's father, MSF contracted the veterans in September with the agreement of The Hague and support of the FSB. At the beginning of December, these veterans were confident in their ability to obtain Arjan Erkel's release in exchange for €180,000 (Arjan later confirmed that around that time he was told yet again by his "keepers" to prepare for imminent release). But, as with the other avenues, the initiative failed due to the political turmoil caused by the arrest in Dagestan of a high-ranking police officer charged with complicity in kidnapping transactions.[54] Describing the sentiment within MSF-Switzerland and the advisory group at the time, the president and the general director of the French section wrote in October 2004:

> After the ultimate failure, in December 2003, a year and a half after the kidnapping of our colleague, we were deeply concerned for his life and completely demoralized by the disappearance of all concrete leads that would advance his liberation. In this period, Mr. Van Wulfften Palthe [a senior official of the Dutch Ministry of Foreign Affairs] recommended that we remain patient, prepare the Erkel family for the worst, and remain silent.[55]

MSF Points to the Direct Responsibility of Russian and Dagestani State Deputies (January–March 2004)

On 14 January 2004, contrary to the advice of the Dutch Ministry of Foreign Affairs the advisory group proposed, in the event no channels worth pursuing emerged by 1 February, to "launch a strong diplomatic/communication strategy in late February/early March". Phase one of the strategy did not differ in that it would continue the objective of maintaining Arjan's international media profile to push for a "safe resolution of the case". Phase two would highlight both the Dutch and Russian governments' "total lack of political will to solve the case", while the third, "*j'accuse*", would be an attack on the Netherlands' lack of commitment and Russia's incompetence or complicity.[56]

While the Geneva crisis cell and steering committee decided to proceed with the plan, the Dutch section remained unconvinced that confronting the Russians was "the only way to do this." Even if the Russian authorities were complicit, "pissing them off is not necessarily going to make them interested in releasing the hostage—it might make them interested in executing the hostage."[57] The Erkel family were even more blunt, holding MSF responsible for Arjan's prolonged detention and threatening legal action if MSF persisted with its communication campaign.[58]

Lukewarm attempts to reassure the Erkel family did not prevent the release of a press pack on 1 March denouncing "the scandal of international complacency" and the "local and regional equilibrium of power and profit" that apparently weighed more than Arjan's life.[59] A sense of urgency was fuelled by the news, received in February, that Arjan was "gravely ill with a chest infection and might well be executed before the upcoming Russian presidential elections, scheduled for March."[60] The press pack was followed up by interviews, notably with the president of the French section acting on behalf of the Geneva crisis cell. Alluding to Vyacheslav Ismailov's investigations, he accused deputies from both Dagestan and the Russian Federation of direct involvement in Arjan's kidnapping.[61] Official reaction was limited to noting that MSF's accusations were "unfounded and far-fetched."[62]

The Veterans—Again (March–April 2004)

Arjan Erkel was finally released on 11 April 2004, one month after the press campaign and MSF's public accusation against Dagestani and Russian officials. The exact circumstances are unclear. Officially, his liberation was described in the Russian press as the result of a "joint operation" carried out by Dagestan's Ministry of the Interior and the local FSB and no further details were provided.[63] According to Arjan's own account, he was transported in the boot of a car from his place of detention to a room at FSB headquarters in Makhachkala where officials told him he was free. He was then shortly debriefed before being flown back to the Netherlands via Moscow. The Dutch minister of foreign affairs claimed credit for the liberation, announcing his government had given the go-ahead for Arjan's release to the same group of FSB veterans it had ended up contracting to negotiate with the kidnappers.[64]

A year and a half on, in contradiction of its own official policy of no negotiating, the Dutch government had finally become actively involved—the Dutch Foreign Ministry said as much during a meeting in Geneva on 25 March 2004 with MSF-Switzerland. Furious once again at MSF's most recent communication campaign, it stated that the "Dutch government has no other choice but to enter into negotiations with Russian authorities". He added, "the Dutch government will send MSF the bill for negotiations in the Arjan issue, whatever the cost will be." And, a few months later, the Dutch government went on to sue MSF in court, asking for reimbursement of the €1 million "service fee" it said it had given in cash to the veterans' association to facilitate Arjan's release.[65]

Dealing with Radical Uncertainty

Twelve years after Arjan Erkel's release, we still do not know the identities of his "takers" (the initial abductors), his "keepers" (those who kept him in detention for 607 days) or his "owners" (those who took the decision to abduct and then release him).

In his memoir, Arjan Erkel describes his "keepers" as Chechen Islamist militants who made repeated reference to the amount of his ransom and to the fact that MSF was not being targeted for its work or past outspokenness.[66] The FSB continued to refrain from commenting on the details of Arjan's release or those responsible, and the head of the veterans referred only vaguely to "criminals, a mixed group of nationalities, including, I think, Chechens." Meanwhile, despite taking credit for Arjan's release, the Dutch government continued to maintain its stance of public discretion, notably with regard to the Russian authorities, and was unable or unwilling to provide details of those responsible.[67]

From MSF's point of view, the prolonged tailing of Arjan, lack of assistance from the FSB agents present during his abduction, shutting down of the investigation, disconnecting of Arjan's mobile phone from which calls had been made after his abduction to FSB and Russian military contacts and the initial lack of a ransom demand despite the proof of life, all contributed to an understanding that, if the Russian authorities had not actually ordered the kidnapping, at the very least they had not put up any opposition. "FSB fingerprints were everywhere—we ended up hiring them", as one member of the advisory group summarised in 2015.[68]

According to most diplomats and specialists on Russia consulted by MSF at the time, intense political pressure was required to secure the involvement of the Russian secret services—an analysis shared across MSF, despite diverging opinions on the public advocacy initiatives.

Despite its official demand for an unconditional release, MSF proved it was ready to obtain Arjan Erkel's freedom at all times and whatever it took. In practice, the crisis cell consistently adopted an approach whereby political pressure was combined with informal proposals to settle the case with a confidential, financial transaction.

However, denouncing the Russian and then the Dutch governments was a particularly difficult decision in view of the opposition of Arjan's family (and, of course, The Hague) to such a strategy. Relations between MSF and the Erkel family were tense right from the start, well before any disagreements surfaced about how to manage the kidnapping. Contributing factors may have included Arjan's father's disapproval of his son working with MSF, but criticism eventually focused on the strategy adopted by MSF-Switzerland, and more especially on the decision to engage in public advocacy, in contradiction of the recommendations of the Dutch government and the security specialists.[69] Apparently convinced that Arjan's captors were simply a gang of criminals and that the Russian authorities were genuinely trying to help, his father interpreted MSF's strategy as a sign of the organisation's lack of professionalism. MSF-Switzerland failed to share with the family its conviction that its strategy was in Arjan's best interests.[70] Its decision to deal with them through an intermediary crisis cell based in Amsterdam, rather than the people directly involved in the negotiations, was a case in point.

So, was Arjan's release facilitated or hindered by the media campaigns? While it may well be impossible to answer this question, there are certain observations based on the chronology of events to be made. The first proof of life and his eventual release occurred within a month of media campaigns. This tends to support the assumptions of the majority of the crisis cell and the advisory group: that the Russian authorities were implicated to the hilt and that they and the Dutch government (with the higher stakes it had with Moscow) would only step in under political pressure.

But, in the view of the head of the Moscow-based crisis cell, the 12 August 2003 campaign was actually counterproductive. The one-year anniversary of the kidnapping represented an important, emblematic selling point for the press and the campaign had acquired a momentum of its own. But the head of the crisis cell considered that, during the potential advances being made in August, it was tactically inopportune to "'poke and prod the beast' while they are trying to help".[71] Given the direct involvement of the FSB in identifying an intermediary—with whom the negotiations appeared to be well underway—this was not the time to upset Russian secret services. Yet, the Geneva crisis cell and the steering committee viewed this lead as insufficiently promising to modify the communication campaign.

Public advocacy was certainly fraught with as many risks as opportunities. That the Russian authorities would react defensively to accusations of "mishandling the investigation and a lack of commitment" goes without saying.[72] More dramatically, pointing the finger at Dagestani and Russian officials could well have endangered Arjan's life. The crisis cell was mindful of this possibility but decided to go ahead. While they were receiving alarming news about his health and threats of execution, and advice from the Dutch government to prepare his family for the worst, they considered that Arjan's life was at greater risk if they just waited.

In the end, this account of Arjan Erkel's abduction and release shows the limits of the technical guidelines and training described in previous chapters of this publication when it comes to dealing with a kidnapping situation. The veil shrouding the identity and motives of the "takers", "keepers", and "owners", and thus the difficulty of assessing the consequences of decisions, generates an uncertainty that cannot be transcended by standardised algorithms and procedures. Ending a hostage situation is less about complying with protocols and more about feeling the way forward, regularly discussing and revising assumptions and decisions while seizing any opportunity to free a colleague as it arises (or for the hostage to escape).[73]

After reading the first draft of this chapter in 2015, the director of operations responsible for taking decisions regarding the affair concluded: "The one thing which is positive is that MSF-Switzerland has always been quite transparent about the dilemmas faced and choices made, which allows us today to discuss the subject openly. In the end, we navigated in very thick fog and in stormy waters until the end and still today we don't know what worked and what didn't. ... We may have to ask the Russians one day!"

NOTES

PREFACE

1. Translated from French by Karen Tucker.

1. HUMANITARIAN SECURITY IN THE AGE OF RISK MANAGEMENT

1. Translated from French by Nina Friedman.
2. See Claude Bruderlein and Pierre Gassmann, "Managing Security Risks in Hazardous Missions: The Challenges of Securing United Nations Access to Vulnerable Groups", *Harvard Human Rights Journal*, vol. 19, 2006, pp. 63–93.
3. Ibid.
4. Such as the Afghanistan NGO Safety Office (ANSO), created in 2002; the NGO Coordination Committee for Iraq (NCCI), formed in 2003; the NGO Safety Project for Somalia, set up in 2004; and the Gaza NGO Safety Office (GANSO), created in 2007.
5. Among them the International NGO Safety and Security Association (INSSA) in the United States (www.ingossa.org) and the European Interagency Security Forum (EISF) in Europe (www.eisf.eu).
6. Such as InterAction's Minimum Operating Security Standards, the Aid Worker Security Database, ODI's *Operational Security Management in Violent Environments* best practice guidelines, and the Security Management Training Course developed by InterAction and RedR with USAID/OFDA support.
7. See for example RedR, which specialises in training, and INSO (International NGO Safety Organisation), which is an NGO entirely devoted to security analysis and consultancy (www.ngosafety.org/about).
8. "Over the past ten to fifteen years, the operational environment of NGOs has become increasingly dangerous. Serious incidents—killings, kidnappings and attacks that cause serious injuries—are on the rise as are politically-motivated attacks against humanitarian workers", InterAction members warned, for example, in 2015 (www.interaction.org/work/security, last accessed 22 December 2015).

9. Mark Duffield, "Risk-Management and the Fortified Aid Compound: Everyday Life in Post-Interventionary Society", *Journal of Intervention and Statebuilding: Working in Challenging Environments*, no. 4 (2010), pp. 453–474; Mark Duffield, Risk Management and Aid Culture in Sudan and Afghanistan Project, November 2011; Mark Duffield, "Challenging Environments: Danger, Resilience and the Aid Industry", *Security Dialogue*, vol. 43, no. 5 (2012), pp. 475–492.

10. Arnaud Dandoy, *Insécurité et aide humanitaire en Haïti: l'impossible dialogue? Décrypter les enjeux des politiques sécuritaires des organisations humanitaires dans l'aire métropolitaine de Port-au-Prince*, Port-au-Prince: Groupe URD, 2013 [authors' translation].

11. The tendency to raise the height of the walls around humanitarian workers—rather than try to do without them—is also central to the critique by researcher Larissa Fast, who encourages aid actors to distance themselves from the dominant security norms in order to re-establish relationships of trust with the populations based on empathy and proximity (see Larissa Fast, *Aid in Danger: The Perils and Promise of Humanitarianism*, Philadelphia: University of Pennsylvania Press, 2014). According to sociologist Silke Roth, loss of motivation and disengagement await humanitarian workers subjected to a security regimen that distances them from the populations and deprives them of autonomy—in particular, the pleasure of taking what they believe to be calculated, justified risks (see "Aid Work as Edgework–Voluntary Risk-Taking and Security in Humanitarian Assistance, Development and Human Rights Work", *Journal of Risk Research*, vol. 18, no. 2 (2015), pp. 139–55.)

12. "Where is everyone? Responding to emergencies in the most difficult places", MSF report, 2014.

13. See Report from MSF-France Head of Mission Week, May 2012; interviews conducted in 2013–2014 with ten programme managers and three operations directors from MSF-France, MSF-Belgium and MSF-Switzerland (Fabrice Weissman, "Sécurité et prise de risques en mission, Synthèse des premiers entretiens", Paris: MSF-CRASH).

14. Claire Magone et al. (eds), *Humanitarian Negotiations Revealed: The MSF Experience*, London: Hurst & Co, 2011.

15. MSF's current charter, dating from 1992, maintains this paragraph in slightly modified form.

16. See Monique J. Beerli, "Securitizing Professions? A Sociology of Humanitarian-Security Professionals and their Practices of Protection", IPS Doctoral Workshop, Ottawa, 25–27 July 2014.

17. Human Security Report Project, *Human Security Report 2009/2010: The Causes of Peace and the Shrinking Costs of War*, New York: Oxford University Press, 2010, p. 121.

18. According to Uppsala University data, the war in Syria is primarily responsible for

the four-fold increase (from about 22,600 to 101,000) in the number of violent deaths due to combat from 2011 to 2014. The year 2014 was the deadliest since the fall of the Berlin Wall, though the death rate was still only half that of an average Cold War year. Therése Pettersson and Peter Wallensteen, "Armed conflicts, 1946–2014", *Journal of Peace Research*, vol. 52, no. 4 (2015), pp. 536–550.

19. Christophe Cornevin, "Les rapts de Français explosent dans le monde", *Le Figaro*, 25 January 2010.

20. Source: WFP Executive Board, *Annual Performance Reports*, 1995 and 2014, http://executiveboard.wfp.org/board-documents, last accessed 22 December 2015.

21. See Mark Duffield, *Global Governance and the New Wars: The Merging of Development and Security*, London: Zed Books, 2001. For an MSF perspective, see Fabrice Weissman (ed.), *In the Shadow of "Just Wars": Violence, Politics, and Humanitarian Action*, London: Hurst & Co., 2004; François Jean and MSF (ed.), *Face aux crises...*, Paris: Collection Pluriel, Hachette, 1993.

22. See Soraya Boudia and Nathalie Jas, "Risk and 'Risk Society' in Historical Perspective", *History and Technology*, vol. 23, no. 4 (2007), pp. 317–331.

23. See Jean-Baptiste Fressoz and Dominique Pestre, "Risque et 'société du risque' depuis deux siècles", in Dominique Bourg et al. (eds), *Du risque à la menace. Penser la catastrophe*, Paris: Presses Universitaires de France, 2013, pp. 19–56.

24. Historian Soraya Boudia explains that the extension of formalised risk management techniques to environmental issues in the United States in the early 1980s followed a similar logic: "to contain the physical and political spillovers caused by activities whose growth [the authorities] deemed inexorable despite their health and environmental costs". The well-known report "Risk Assessment in the Federal Government: Managing the Process" (considered the "bible" on the subject) was based on research funded by the RAND Corporation and the Ford Foundation, in the wake of mounting environmental protests around oil spills, pesticides and nuclear power. They used studies from cognitive psychology on the perception of risk and how to render it acceptable to the public, and econometric studies basing risk management on the calculation of cost–benefit ratios. See Soraya Boudia, "La genèse d'un gouvernement par le risque", in ibid., pp. 57–76.

25. See on this subject Michel Tondellier, "L'action organisée face à la prise de risque: l'héroïsme au travail et son institutionnalisation", Acteur, risque et prise de risque colloque, CNRS, Lille, 2004; Patrick Le Gal, "L'esprit de sacrifice dans l'armée professionnelle d'aujourd'hui", in Christian Benoit et al. (eds), *Le sacrifice du soldat. Corps martyrisé, corps mythifié*, Paris: CNRS Éditions, 2009, pp. 56–59.

26. According to sociologist Patrick Peretti-Watel, the contemporary mindset is marked by what sociologist Jean Kellerhals calls "providentialism", i.e., the "primacy of the individual's concern for protection against the social environment, and even against the consequences of his own decisions." Demanding protection

147

and looking for accountability when the former is lacking relates to what Giddens calls the "disembedding of social relations"—the fact that increasing interactions render us dependent on complex technical systems vouched for by professionals. In this regard, the pursuit of accountability reflects not just the new individualism, but also the public's protest against the power of the experts and authorities upon whom it increasingly depends. See Patrick Peretti-Watel, *La société du risque*, Paris: La Découverte, 2010, pp. 47–50.

27. See Michael Power, *The Audit Society: Rituals of Verification*, Oxford: Oxford University Press, 1997; Michael Power, *Organized Uncertainty: Designing a World of Risk Management*, Oxford: Oxford University Press, 2007.

28. Imogen Wall, "NRC kidnap ruling is 'wake-up' call for aid industry", IRIN News, 25 November 2015, http://www.irinnews.org/report/102243/nrc-kidnap-ruling-is-wake-up-call-for-aid-industry

29. As a reminder, MSF is an international movement with five operational sections and sixteen partner sections.

30. Harmer et al., *Good Practice Review: Operational Security Management in Violent Environments*, Humanitarian Practice Network, London: Overseas Development Institute, revised edition, 2010, xviii.

31. See Chapter 3, p. 37.

32. Harmer et al., op. cit., p. 159.

33. He continues: "The notion of risk then appears as a reducer of uncertainty, characteristic of the prospective activity of an individual who seeks to control his future or that of others, like an insurer or actuary. Risk is, in a word, a danger that proliferates, insofar as the notion leads to the multiplication, and thus dispersal, of causal links." Peretti-Watel, op. cit., pp. 14–15 [authors' translation].

34. See Fabrice Weissman, "Silence Heals...", in Claire Magone et al. (eds), op. cit.

35. Dominique Genelot and Jean-Louis Le Moigne, *Manager dans la complexité: Réflexions à l'usage des dirigeants*, 4th edition, Paris: INSEP Consulting, 2011.

36. Vincent Desportes, *Décider dans l'incertitude*, 2nd ed. Paris: Economica, 2015. Carl von Clausewitz used the phrase "fog of war" to describe the unreliability of the information available to officers: "In war, much of the information is contradictory, even more is false, and the majority is uncertain; the facts are rarely fully known and their motivations even less so." (cited in Desportes, p. 37). "Friction" refers to the "countless minor incidents—of the kind you cannot really foresee—[that] combine to reduce the general level of effectiveness in such a way that one never achieves the goal" (von Clausewitz, cited in Desportes, pp. 38–39) [authors' translation].

37. Koenraad Van Brabant, "Mainstreaming the Organisational Management of Safety and Security: A review of aid agency practices and a guide for management", HPG Report 9, London: Overseas Development Institute, March 2001, p. 17.

38. Harmer et al., op. cit., p. 123.

39. Van Brabant, op. cit., p. 49.
40. Béatrice Hibou, *La bureaucratisation néolibérale*, Paris: La Découverte, 2013.
41. Hibou gives the example of a nurse who spends a third of her workday documenting it on standardised forms—a large percentage of which were created by non-medical consultants—and who, once home, must battle the various formalities necessary to manage her telephone subscription and other day-to-day bureaucratic obligations, the sense of which escape her. Hibou, op. cit., pp. 5–14.
42. See François Giovalucchi and Jean-Pierre Olivier de Sardan, "Planification, gestion et politique dans l'aide au développement: le cadre logique, outil et miroir des développeurs", *Revue Tiers Monde* no. 198 (2009/2), pp. 383.
43. Studying the logical framework's impact on development practices, Giovalucchi and Olivier de Sardan underscore the contrast between its ideological hegemony and its limited use in practice. They explain: "the ideological meanings or cognitive assumptions incorporated to varying degrees in the tool can be applied, ignored, transformed, bypassed or manipulated in actual practice. Thus, a rigorous analysis [of the tool] as an instrument of public action should both reveal the political ideology and cognitive model embedded in it and describe its practical uses." Ibid. [authors' translation].
44. While the UN has encouraged honouring "those who have lost their lives in humanitarian service" on 19 August every year since 2008, the number of monuments dedicated to humanitarian workers who died on mission has been growing in recent years (especially in Great Britain, Canada and Australia). In addition, awareness campaigns condemning violence against aid workers (the ICRC's "Health Care in Danger" campaign, or ACF's "Protect Aid Workers" campaign) participate in the symbolic transformation of humanitarian workers into the heroes and martyrs of contemporary wars. Yet as anthropologist Jean-Pierre Albert writes, "the heroism is linked not to the outcome of the undertaking, but to the acceptance of risk and suffering, even death." Thus, paradoxically, the spirit of sacrifice associated with the chivalrous ethos of the early humanitarians is co-opted to rationalise exposure to danger based on actuarial cost–benefit calculations. See Jean-Pierre Albert, "Du martyr à la star. Les métamorphoses des héros nationaux", in Pierre Centlivres et al. (eds), *La Fabrique des héros*, Paris: Éditions de la Maison des Sciences de l'Homme, 1998.
45. In this sense, humanitarian action belongs to the domain of prudential occupations described by Florent Champy, from whom we borrow the observations that follow. See Florent Champy, "Grand résumé de *Nouvelle théorie sociologique des professions*, Paris: Presses Universitaires de France, 2011", *SociologieS*, 9 May 2012, http://sociologies.revues.org/3922, last accessed 22 December 2015.
46. Ibid.

2. ON DANGER, SACRIFICE AND PROFESSIONALISATION: MSF AND THE SECURITY DEBATE

1. Translated from French by Nina Friedman.
2. This analysis concerns only MSF's French section.
3. Bernard Kouchner, *Le malheur des autres*, Paris: Odile Jacob, 1992 (1st ed. 1991), p. 322 [translated].
4. For an account of the origins of the engagement of MSF's founders, see Eleanor Davey, *Idealism Beyond Borders. The French Revolutionary Left and the Rise of Humanitarianism, 1954–1988*, Cambridge: Cambridge University Press, 2015.
5. Médecins Sans Frontières, President's Report, 1977 General Assembly [translated].
6. Médecins Sans Frontières, President's Report, 1980 General Assembly [translated].
7. Médecins Sans Frontières, President's Report, 1981 General Assembly [translated].
8. Médecins Sans Frontières, Collegial Steering Committee, 18 July 1981 [translated].
9. Médecins Sans Frontières, President's Report, 1981 General Assembly [translated].
10. Interview with Rony Brauman, 6 October 2014.
11. Médecins Sans Frontières, President's Report, 1987 General Assembly [translated].
12. Médecins Sans Frontières, President's Report, 1984 General Assembly [translated].
13. Médecins Sans Frontières, President's Report, 1982 General Assembly [translated].
14. Four MSF and two AMI hospitals were hit between 1981 and March 1982.
15. Médecins Sans Frontières, Board of Directors, 15 September 1989 [translated].
16. Médecins Sans Frontières, President's Report, 1989 General Assembly [translated].
17. Médecins Sans Frontières, Board of Directors, 20 May 1994 [translated].
18. Mark Duffield, "Challenging Environments: Danger, Resilience and the Aid Industry," in *Security Dialogue*, vol. 43, no. 5, 2012, pp. 475–492.
19. "Security of relief workers and humanitarian space", Commission working document, EU Commission, May 1998.
20. On this discourse and criticisms of it, see Roland Marchal and Christine Messiant, "Les guerres civiles à l'ère de la globalisation", *Critique Internationale*, no. 18 (2003/1), pp. 91–112.
21. Final Communiqué of the Denver Summit of the Eight, 22 June 1997, www.library. utoronto.ca/g7/summit/1997denver/g8final.htm, last accessed 22 December 2015.

NOTES pp. [27–31]

22. EU Commission, op. cit.
23. Koenraad Van Brabant, "Security Guidelines: no guarantee for improved security", Humanitarian Practice Network, London: Overseas Development Institute, February 1997.
24. Ibid.
25. Franck Schmidt, "Recommendations for improving the security of humanitarian workers," *International Review of the Red Cross*, vol. 37, no. 317 (1997), pp. 152–155.
26. The integration of stress was anything but anecdotal. It showed the importance that the psychological health of staff having to contend with violence was beginning to have in the humanitarian sector.
27. InterAction's Security Advisory Group (1991), Inter-Agency Security Management Network (1994).
28. See, in particular, Larissa Fast, *Aid in Danger. The Perils and Promise of Humanitarianism*, Philadelphia: University of Pennsylvania Press, 2014.
29. See, in particular, Gérald Massis (ed.), *Manuel de l'administrateur/logisticien*, Médecins Sans Frontières, 1990.
30. Médecins Sans Frontières, President's Report, 1992 General Assembly [translated].
31. Médecins Sans Frontières, Board of Directors, 24 November 1995 [translated].
32. Médecins Sans Frontières, Board of Directors, 28 June 1996 [translated].
33. Ibid.
34. Ibid.
35. Interview with Brigitte Vasset, former director of operations of MSF-France, 1 December 2014 [translated].
36. Médecins Sans Frontières, Board of Directors, 28 June 1996 [translated].
37. Médecins Sans Frontières, Board of Directors, 30 June 1995 [translated].
38. For a partial analysis of this professionalisation movement, see Claudine Vidal and Jacques Pinel, "MSF 'Satellites'" in Jean-Hervé Bradol and Claudine Vidal (eds), *Medical Innovations in Humanitarian Situations: The Work of Médecins Sans Frontières*, New York: Médecins Sans Frontières, 2011.
39. Médecins Sans Frontières, President's Report, 1991 General Assembly [translated].
40. Médecins Sans Frontières, President's Report, 1993 General Assembly [translated].
41. Médecins Sans Frontières, President's Report, 1998 General Assembly [translated].
42. See, for example, Médecins Sans Frontières, Board of Directors, 11 July 1997; 30 October 1998; and 29 January 1999.
43. Interview with Marc Gastellu-Etchegorry, former director of the emergency unit of MSF-France, 3 February 2015.

44. Fabrice Weissman, "Quelle place pour les organisations humanitaires en situation de conflit?" *L'état du monde 2015: Nouvelles guerres*, Paris: Éditions La découverte, 2014.

45. "Introduction" in Claire Magone et al. (eds), *Humanitarian Negotiations Revealed: The MSF Experience*, London: Hurst & Co., 2011.

46. Fast, op. cit.

47. See http://www.un.org/en/events/humanitarianday/, last accessed 22 December 2015.

48. See Chapter 4, p. 55.

49. See Chapter 5, p. 71.

50. See Chapter 8, p. 127.

51. See Chapter 5, box: "Who Benefits From 'Duty of Care?'", p. 82.

52. Note that while references to the principles contained in the "golden rules" were everywhere in the discussions, the term itself disappeared from mention.

53. See, in particular, Fabrice Weissman, "Military Humanitarianism: A Deadly Confusion," in the International Activity Report 2003–2004, Paris: MSF.

54. Médecins Sans Frontières, President's Report, 2000 General Assembly [translated].

55. Médecins Sans Frontières, Board of Directors, 24 April 2003 [translated].

56. Ibid.

57. Médecins Sans Frontières, Board of Directors, 29 October 2004 [translated].

58. Médecins Sans Frontières, Board of Directors, 25 October 2002 [translated].

59. Médecins Sans Frontières, Board of Directors, 24 April 2003 [translated].

60. Médecins Sans Frontières, Board of Directors, 28 March 2003 [translated].

61. Médecins Sans Frontières, Board of Directors, 30 September 2004 [translated].

62. Médecins Sans Frontières, Board of Directors, 29 August 2008 [translated].

63. Médecins Sans Frontières, Board of Directors, 27 February 2009 [translated].

64. Médecins Sans Frontières, President's Report, 2003 General Assembly [translated].

65. Médecins Sans Frontières, Board of Directors, 27 February 2009 [translated].

66. Médecins Sans Frontières, Joint Board meeting, 27 January 2012.

67. Médecins Sans Frontières, Joint Board meeting, 6–7 December 2013.

3. DANGER, RISK, SECURITY AND PROTECTION: CONCEPTS AT THE HEART OF THE HISTORY OF HUMANITARIAN AID

1. This article is based on two ESRC-funded research projects: UN Data ES/L007479/1 and Selling Compassion ES/I031359/1. It was presented as a paper at the Humanitarian Studies Association conference in Istanbul in 2013, in a paper version at MSF-France in Paris and at the Humanitarian Congress in Berlin in 2014. Thanks to all the collaborators and colleagues involved, Roger MacGinty, Róisín

Read, Julie-Marie Strange, Sarah Roddy, Michaël Neuman and Fabrice Weissman, for their support in the research and writing.

2. A. H. Smee and Thomas G. Ackland, "On the Assurance Risks Incident to Professional Military and Naval Lives; and the Rates of Extra Premiums Which Should be Charged for Such Risks. Being Extracts from a Joint Report, made in May 1890, to the Board of Directors of the Gresham Life Assurance Society," *Journal of the Institute of Actuaries*, vol. 34, no. 4, 1899, pp. 358–385.

3. Bill Luckin and Roger Cooter (eds), *Accidents in History: Injuries, Fatalities and Social Relations*, Amsterdam: Clio Medica, 1997.

4. William K. Sessions, *They Chose the Star: Quaker War Relief Work in France, 1870–1875*, York: Sessions Books, 1991.

5. Graham Benjamin et al., *Security Analysis*, New York: McGraw-Hill, 1934; Ingvar Laurin, "An Introduction into Lundberg's Theory of Risk", *Scandinavian Actuarial Journal* no. 1, 1930, pp. 84–111; William O. Douglas, "Vicarious Liability and Administration of Risk I.", *Yale Law Journal* no. 38, 1928, p. 584.

6. Joseph Brown, "The evils of the unlimited liability for accidents of masters and railway companies, especially since Lord Campbell's act: a paper read before the Social Science Association", *Butterworths*, 1870.

7. William Colebrooke, "Negligence in Imminent Peril", *American Law Register* (1886), pp. 617–632.

8. J. S. S. "The Doctrine of Last Clear Chance in Virginia", *Virginia Law Review*, vol. 40, no. 5, 1954, pp. 666–680.

9. Huey B. Howerton Jr, "Tort Liability for Failure to Assist Others in Peril", *Mississippi Law Journal* no. 16, 1943, p. 379.

10. Will D. Davis, "Doctrine of Discovered Peril", *Baylor Law Review*, no. 6, 1953, p. 61.

11. The word "humanitarian" refers here to the spirit of the doctrine—one concerned with the welfare of victims—rather than to humanitarian work in our current understanding. This nevertheless illustrates how plastic and widespread the concept of humanitarianism was before it became the preserve of humanitarian organisations or international humanitarian law.

12. The archives of Stafford House are to be found at the Staffordshire County Record Office (SCRO) in the private papers of Lord Sutherland. See Sarah Roddy et al., *Selling Compassion*, forthcoming.

13. Stafford House Committee for the Relief of Sick and Wounded Turkish Soldiers, *Report and Record of the Operations of the Stafford House Committee, Russo Turkish War, 1877–78*, London: Spottiswoode & Co, 1879.

14. *Evening Standard*, 2 September 1877; SCRO D593/P/26/2/7.

15. See Max Jones, *The Last Great Quest: Captain Scott's Antarctic Sacrifice*, Oxford: Oxford University Press, 2004; Max Jones et al., 'Decolonising imperial heroes: Britain and France.' *The Journal of Imperial and Commonwealth History*, vol. 42, no. 5, 2014, pp. 787–825.

16. Andrew Porter, "Sir Roger Casement and the international humanitarian movement", *The Journal of Imperial and Commonwealth History*, vol. 29, no. 2, 2001, pp. 59–74.

17. Bruno Cabanes, *The Great War and the Origins of Humanitarianism, 1918–1924*, Cambridge: Cambridge University Press, 2014, pp. 133–188.

18. Interview with Jacques Pinel, 7 March 2013.

19. For instance R. B. Macpherson, *Under the Red Crescent; Or Ambulance Adventures in the Russo-Turkish War of 1877–78*, rare book club reprint, 2012. The language of adventure recurs throughout humanitarian writings; see for instance Jean-Christophe Rufin, *L'Aventure humanitaire*, Paris: Gallimard, 1994.

20. Rebecca Gill, *Calculating Compassion*, Manchester: Manchester University Press, 2013, pp. 63–5.

21. Bertrand Taithe, "Horror, Abjection and Compassion: From Dunant to Compassion Fatigue", *New Formations*, no. 62 (2007), pp. 123–36.

22. J. Henry Dunant, *A Memory of Solferino. 1862*, Washington D.C.: American National Red Cross, 1939.

23. Jean-Charles Chenu, *De la mortalité dans l'armée et des moyens d'économiser la vie humaine*, Paris: Hachette, 1870; Claire Fredj, "Compter les morts de Crimée: un tournant sur l'identité professionnelle des médecins de l'armée française (1865–1882)", *Histoire, économie & société*, vol. 29, no. 3, 2010, pp. 95–108.

24. Stafford House Committee for the Relief of Sick and Wounded Turkish Soldiers, *Report and Record of the Operations of the Stafford House Committee, Russo Turkish War, 1877–78*, London: Spottiswoode & Co, 1879, p. 40. For the same period, seven had died of the forty-five working for the Red Crescent; in the British Red Cross, three out of fourteen were ill.

25. "Aid for the wounded".

26. Anon., *Les violations de la convention de Genève par les Français en 1870–1871*, Berlin: Charles Duncker, 1871; J. M. Félix Christot, *Le Massacre de l'ambulance de Saône-et-Loire le 21 janvier 1871; Rapport lu au Comité médical de secours aux blessés le 7 juillet 1871*, Lyon: Vingtrinier, 1871; Charles Aimé Dauban, *La Guerre comme la font les Prussiens*, Paris: Plon, 1870; Bertrand Taithe, *Defeated Flesh: Welfare, Warfare and the Making of Modern France*, Manchester: Manchester University Press, 1999, pp. 169–73.

27. Stafford House Committee for the Relief of Sick and Wounded Turkish Soldiers, *Report and Record of the Operations of the Stafford House Committee, Russo Turkish War, 1877–78*, London: Spottiswoode & Co, 1879, p. 50.

28. MacPherson, op. cit., p. 17.

29. Teresa Eden Pearce-Serocold Richardson, *In Japanese Hospitals During War-time: Fifteen Months with the Red Cross Society of Japan (April 1904 to July 1905)*, New York: W. Blackwood and Sons, 1905; Philip A. Towle, "Japanese Treatment of Prisoners in 1904–1905: Foreign Officers' Reports", *Military Affairs: The Journal of Military History* (1975), pp. 115–118.

30. Caroline Reeves, "Sovereignty and the Chinese Red Cross Society: The Differentiated Practice of International Law in Shandong, 1914–1916", *Journal of the History of International Law/Revue d'histoire du droit international*, vol. 13, no. 1, 2011, pp. 155–177.

31. Maria del Carmen Pérez-Aguado et al., "Medicine and nursing in the Spanish Civil War: women who served in the health services of the International Brigades (1936–1939)", *Vesalius* (2010) Suppl: 29–33.

32. These terms are used in their current anthropological meaning to denote power over access and exchanges.

33. 3rd Duke of Sutherland, preface, "Report and Record of the Operations of the Stafford House Committee for the Relief of Sick and Wounded Turkish Soldiers", p. 4.

34. See Mark Micale and Paul Lerner (eds), *Traumatic Pasts: History, Psychiatry and Trauma in the Modern Age, 1870–1930*, Cambridge: Cambridge University Press, 2010, pp. 2–27.

35. MacPherson, op. cit., p. 119.

36. In that regard, there are a lot of commonalities with the early ages of MSF. See Chapter 2, p. 21.

37. M. C. Lüder, *La Convention de Genève au point de vue pratique, théorique et dogmatique*, Erlangen: E. Besold, 1876.

38. Bertrand Taithe, op. cit., pp. 75–90.

39. Jacques Meurant, "Inter Arma Caritas: Evolution and Nature of International Humanitarian Law", *Journal of Peace Research*, vol. 24, no. 3, 1987, pp. 237–249.

40. André Durand, "Le premier Prix Nobel de la Paix (1901): Candidatures d'Henry Dunant, de Gustave Moynier et du Comité international de la Croix-Rouge", *Revue Internationale de la Croix-Rouge/International Review of the Red Cross*, no. 842, pp. 275–285.

41. See Chapter 1, p. 1.

42. Davide Rodogno, *Against Massacre: Humanitarian Interventions in the Ottoman Empire, 1815–1914*, Princeton: Princeton University Press, 2011; Alexis Heraclides and Ada Dialla, *Humanitarian Intervention in the Long Nineteenth Century*, Manchester: Manchester University Press, 2015.

43. James Orbinski, *Le cauchemar humanitaire*, Marne-la-Vallée: Music & Entertainment Books, 2010, p. 99.

44. Lisa Smirl, *Spaces of Aid: How Cars, Compounds and Hotels Shape Humanitarianism*, London: Zed Books, 2015.

45. Mark Duffield, "Risk Management and the Fortified Aid Compound: Everyday Life in Post-Interventionary Society," *Journal of Intervention and Statebuilding*, vol. 4, no. 4, 2010, pp. 453–474; Mark Duffield, "Challenging Environments: Danger, Resilience and the Aid Industry," *Security Dialogue*, vol. 43, no. 5, 2012, pp. 475–492.

46. See Chapter 4, box "Security Incident Narrative Buried in Numbers: The MSF Example", p. 67.

47. See Chapter 5, p. 71.

48. Amadou Hampâté Bâ, *The Fortunes of Wangrin*, Bloomington: Indiana University Press, 1999; Ralph A. Austen, "Colonialism from the Middle: African Clerks as Historical Actors and Discursive Subjects", *History in Africa*, no. 38, 2011, pp. 21–33.

49. Ann Laura Stoler, "Rethinking Colonial Categories: European Communities and the Boundaries of Rule", *Comparative Studies in Society and History*, vol. 31, no. 1, 1989, pp. 134–161; Benjamin Nicholas Lawrance et al. (eds), *Intermediaries, Interpreters, and Clerks: African Employees in the Making of Colonial Africa*, Madison: University of Wisconsin Press, 2006.

50. Kenneth Cain et al., *Emergency Sex and Other Desperate Measures*, London: Ebury Press, 2005.

51. Lebanon intervention by the Franco-British fleet in response to Druze massacres of Maronite Lebanese. Istvan Pogany, "Humanitarian Intervention in International Law: The French Intervention in Syria Re-Examined", *International and Comparative Law Quarterly*, vol. 35, no. 1, 1986, pp. 182–190.

52. See Chapter 4, p. 55.

4. VIOLENCE AGAINST AID WORKERS: THE MEANING OF MEASURING

1. Translated from French by Nina Friedman.

2. Patrick Brugger, "ICRC operational security: staff safety in armed conflict and internal violence", *International Review of the Red Cross*, no. 874 (2009), p. 431.

3. Robin Coupland, "The Role of Health-Related Data in Promoting the Security of Health Care in Armed Conflict and Other Emergencies", *International Review of the Red Cross*, no. 889 (2013), p. 61.

4. Mani Sheik et al., "Deaths among Humanitarian Workers", *British Medical Journal*, 321 (2000), pp. 166–68.

5. Cate Buchanan and Robert Muggah, "No Relief: Surveying the effects of gun violence on humanitarian and development personnel", Geneva: Centre for Humanitarian Dialogue, Small Arms Survey, June 2005.

6. Elizabeth A. Rowley et al., "Violence-Related Mortality and Morbidity of Humanitarian Workers", *American Journal of Disaster Medicine*, vol. 3, no. 1, 2008, pp. 39–45.

7. See https://aidworkersecurity.org/, last accessed 29 December 2015.

8. Abby Stoddard et al., "Providing Aid in Insecure Environments: Trends in Policy and Operations", HPG Report 23, London: Overseas Development Institute, 2006.

9. See https://aidworkersecurity.org/citations, last accessed 29 December 2015.

10. See www.insecurityinsight.org, last accessed 29 December 2015.

11. Christina Wille, "The six 'Ws' of security policy-making", *Humanitarian Exchange Magazine*, no. 47, 2010, pp. 6–8.

12. ICRC, "Health care in danger: a sixteen-country study", Geneva: ICRC, 2011; ICRC, "Violent Incidents Affecting Health Care. January to December 2012", Geneva: ICRC, 2013.

13. See https://aidworkersecurity.org/about, last accessed 29 December 2015.

14. These obstacles are comparable to those encountered when quantifying crime in France, for example. See Renée Zauberman et al., "L'acteur et la mesure: Le comptage de la délinquance entre données administratives et enquêtes", *Revue française de sociologie*, vol. 50, no. 1, 2009, p. 31.

15. Koenraad Van Brabant, an advocate of professionalised humanitarian security, observes that there is much resistance when introducing security data collection, due to the fact that it might bring professional errors to light, tarnish the image of certain operations and jeopardise their existence, as well as the funding and employment contracts that depend on them. Koenraad Van Brabant, "Incident Statistics in Aid Worker Safety and Security Management: Using and Producing Them", London: European Interagency Security Forum, 2012.

16. As the French national observatory for violence in healthcare settings (*Observatoire national des violences en milieu de santé*, or ONVS, created in 2005) writes [translation]: "the number of reports does not reflect how dangerous a healthcare site is, but rather the number of times professionals felt it important to report. This varies widely from one facility to another, from one department to another and, at a given healthcare site, from one year to another (...). Raw data have little meaning in themselves, but illustrate situations experienced in the facilities, the awareness of the actors and the promotion of preventive actions". See "Observatoire national des violences en milieu de santé. Rapport annuel 2012", Paris: Ministry of Social Affairs and Health, January 2013, p. 3.

17. See Chapter 6, box, "The Case of 'Dangerous Patients' in Yemen's Governorate of Amran", p. 103. Similarly the French national observatory for violence in healthcare settings notices that two different facilities report as "serious assault on the physical integrity of health personnel" the following events [translation]: "while saying hello, the patient shook violently my left wrist. I asked him to stop, he did not. I screamed and the staff arrived"; and "when putting the patient in an isolation room, he pulled out a knife. We just had time to close the door. He refused to drop the knife and threatened with death the health assistant and other staff members." Ibid.

18. See www.humanitarianoutcomes.org/gdho/methodology, last accessed 29 December 2015.

19. Christina Wille and Larissa Fast, "Operating in Insecurity: Shifting patterns of violence against humanitarian aid providers and their staff (1996–2010)", Switzerland: Insecurity Insight, 2013, p. 3.

20. Sheik et al., op. cit., p. 167.

21. Coupland, op. cit., p. 65.

22. Sheik et al., op. cit., p. 167.

23. See https://aidworkersecurity.org/, last accessed 29 December 2015.

24. Wille and Fast, op. cit., p. 3.

25. Sheik et al., op. cit., pp. 166–68.

26. Abby Stoddard et al., "Unsafe Passage: Road attacks and their impact on humanitarian operations", Aid Worker Security Report 2014, London: Humanitarian Outcomes, August 2014, p. 2.

27. See https://aidworkersecurity.org/incidents/report/rates, last accessed 29 December 2015.

28. Stoddard et al., "Providing Aid in Insecure Environments", op. cit.

29. Abby Stoddard et al., "Providing Aid in Insecure Environments: 2009 Update", HPG Policy Brief No. 34, London: Overseas Development Institute, 2009.

30. Adele Harmer et al., "The New Normal: Coping with the kidnapping threat", Humanitarian Security Report 2013, London: Humanitarian Outcomes, October 2013.

31. This figure is of the same order as the risk of violent incidents causing death or injuries estimated by Johns Hopkins to be six per 10,000 per year between 2002 and 2005. Rowley et al., op. cit.

32. HO's consultants justify the way they present their results with the need to produce reports that are "a kind of reminder to political actors that humanitarian aid work is quite a dangerous job" (interview with a senior Humanitarian Outcomes consultant, 16 April 2015).

33. See https://aidworkersecurity.org/incidents/report/rates, 29 December 2015.

34. Stoddard et al., "Providing Aid in Insecure Environments", op. cit.

35. Harmer et al., op. cit.

36. In 2014, the violence was even more concentrated, with three-quarters occurring in Afghanistan, Pakistan, Syria and the two Sudans.

37. Abby Stoddard et al., "Host States and Their Impact on Security for Humanitarian Operations", Aid Worker Security Report 2012, London: Humanitarian Outcomes, December 2012, p. 4.

38. U.S. Bureau of Labor Statistics, U.S. Department of Labor, 2015, www.bls.gov/iif/oshwc/cfoi/cfch0012.pdf, last accessed 29 December 2015.

39. Abby Stoddard et al., "Spotlight on security for national aid workers: Issues and perspectives", Aid Worker Security Report 2011, Humanitarian Outcomes, August 2011, p. 3.

40. Wille and Fast, op. cit., p. 23.

41. Stoddard et al., "Providing Aid in Insecure Environments", op. cit., p. 19.

42. Stoddard et al., "Spotlight on Security for National Aid Workers", op. cit., p. 3.

43. Stoddard et al., "Providing Aid in Insecure Environments", op. cit., p. 19.

44. Ibid., p. 1.

45. Stoddard et al., "Unsafe Passage", op. cit., p. 6.

46. Stoddard et al., "Providing Aid in Insecure Environments: 2009 update", op. cit., pp. 5–6.

47. Claire Magone et al. (eds), *Humanitarian Negotiations Revealed: The MSF Experience*, London: Hurst & Co, 2012.

48. Arnaud Dandoy and Marc-Antoine Pérouse de Montclos, "Humanitarian Workers in Peril? Deconstructing the myth of the new and growing threat to humanitarian workers", *Global Crime*, vol. 14, no. 4, 2013, pp. 341–58.

49. See Chapter 3, p. 67.

50. See Chapter 1, p. 1.

51. Quote attributed to Albert Einstein, taken from Christine Fassert, "'Tout ce qui compte ne peut être compté': la (non-) fabrication d'un indicateur de sécurité dans le contrôle aérien", *Sociologie et sociétés*, vol. 43, no. 2, 2011, p. 249.

52. Coupland, op. cit., p. 66.

53. On the humanitarian exceptionalism construct, see Larissa Fast, *Aid in Danger: The Perils and Promise of Humanitarianism*, Philadelphia: University of Pennsylvania Press, 2014.

54. Coupland, op. cit., p. 66.

55. Didier Fassin and Patrice Bourdelais (eds), *Les constructions de l'intolérable. Études d'anthropologie et d'histoire sur les frontières de l'espace moral*, Paris: La Découverte, 2005.

56. ICRC, "Violent Incidents Affecting Health Care: January to December 2012", op. cit., p. 2 n. 5.

57. In the words of social philosopher Alasdair MacIntyre, "seeking a unified theory of violent behaviour makes no more sense than seeking a single explanation for quick behaviour." Just as there is an infinite variety of reasons for doing things quickly, there is an infinite variety of reasons for behaving violently toward a person working (or not) for a relief organisation. See *Human Security Report 2013— The Decline in Global Violence: Evidence, Explanation, and Contestation*, Simon Fraser University, Vancouver: Human Security Research Group, 2014, p. 42.

58. Translated from French by Justin Hillier.

59. On 20 June 1997, an MSF-France doctor was murdered at a hospital in Baidoa by the comrade of a hospitalised militiaman who had died the previous day. On 28 January 2008, a surgeon and a logistician working for MSF-Holland were killed along with their driver when the vehicle they were travelling in was hit by a remote-controlled bomb in Kismayo. On 29 December 2011, MSF-Belgium's head of mission and a medical coordinator were killed in their office in Mogadishu by a recently fired employee.

60. On 28 April 1990, an MSF-France logistician was killed in an advanced medical post in Yaftal in Badakhshan. On 2 June 2004, a project coordinator, doctor and

logistician working for MSF-Holland died with their driver and translator when local fighters in Baghdis province opened fire on their car with automatic weapons.

61. On 21 December 1989, an Aviation Sans Frontières plane was shot down while taking off from Aweil, killing its pilot and three passengers: a doctor and a logistician working for MSF-France and a World Food Programme technician.

62. On 13 November 1992, an MSF-Belgium logistician died from his wounds after being attacked during an armed burglary.

63. On 11 June 2007, an MSF-France logistician died from her wounds after her car was ambushed, apparently mistakenly, by rebels in the Ngaoundai region in northwest Central African Republic.

64. See Chapter 5, p. 71.

65. "Safety & Security Incidents & Accidents" database, MSF-Belgium, Brussels, 15 December 2009.

66. For example, a head of mission can only look up incidents that occurred in the country where he or she works, whereas the director of operations and the security advisor have rights to the entire database.

67. Using a standard form to which any type of document can be attached.

68. SINDY's interface requests a user to describe each incident, guided by fields and drop-down menus with pre-determined options: location; time; weapon(s) used; type of tactical situation (ambush, gunfire, bombing, etc.); types of violence (armed, sexual, etc.); victim profile; mission profile; financial, human and operational impact; crisis management procedure implemented, etc.

69. Each incident logged in the database triggers an email notification sent to all subscribers.

70. MSF-France classifies as "severe" any violent action against MSF staff, patient or property causing death or serious injury (incapacity to work), rape, kidnapping, theft and material damage valued at €10,000 or more. "Moderate" describes incidents that had the potential to become a severe incident (threats or near-miss incidents) and any other incident the field deemed important to log in the database (to keep a record and share easily, notify the chain of command, etc.) OCP (Operational Centre Paris) SINDY User Manual, Paris: MSF, November 2013, p. 8.

71. SINDY 2, Security Focal Point, Brussels: MSF-OCB (Operational Centre Brussels), December 2010, p. 3.

72. OCA (Operational Centre Amsterdam), Comparison of Severity Classification of Security Incidents between OCs with the idea to streamline between sections, May 2015.

73. Overview of OCB Risk Management (SINDY 2014 Report), Brussels: MSF-OCB, November 2014, p. 2.

74. Overview of OCA Security Incidents (SINDY 2014 Report), Amsterdam: MSF-OCA, February 2015, p. 7.

75. Overview of OCB Risk Management (SINDY 2014 Report), Brussels: MSF-OCB, November 2014, p. 8.
76. See Chapter 4, p. 55.
77. The bias identified by the security advisors (in the knowledge that SINDY quantifies the number of security incidents entered in the database and not the "actual" number of incidents that occur) has been confirmed several times during observations in the field. A study carried out by MSF in Yemen in 2013 showed that the decision to record incidents in SINDY (particularly less serious ones) varied according to whether the person in charge of inputting this data was at the start or end of their mission and whether or not they wished to notify the office in the capital and head office. See Chapter 6, box: "The Case of 'Dangerous Patients' in Yemen's Governorate of Amran", p. 103.
78. See Eric Marsden (ed.), "Quelques bonnes questions à se poser sur son dispositif REX", Les Cahiers de la sécurité industrielle 2014–01, Fondation pour une Culture de Sécurité Industrielle, pp. 23, https://www.foncsi.org/fr/publications/collections/cahiers-securite-industrielle/bonnes-questions-REX/CSI-REX-bonnes-questions.pdf/view, last accessed 29 December 2015.
79. Fassert, op. cit., pp. 249–272.
80. Also could be included: "number of days detained", "number of vehicles stolen/returned", "value of property destroyed or stolen".
81. http://www.bea.aero/fr/bea/information/information.php. See http://www.bea.aero/fr/bea/information/information.php, last accessed 29 December 2015.

5. HUMANITARIAN SECURITY MANUALS: NEUTRALISING THE HUMAN FACTOR IN HUMANITARIAN ACTION

1. David Lloyd Roberts, *Staying Alive: Safety and Security Guidelines for Humanitarian Volunteers in Conflict Areas*, Geneva: ICRC, 1999.
2. Mark Cutts and Alan Dingle, *Safety First: Protecting NGO Employees Who Work in Areas of Conflict*, 2nd ed., London: Save the Children, 1998.
3. At the beginning of the 1990s, as part of a general guideline on administrative and logistical issues, MSF also established its first set of security "Golden Rules", along with practical recommendations on how to build a bomb shelter, move around and manage communications in insecure environments. See Chapter 2, p. 21.
4. Koenraad Van Brabant, *Good Practice Review 8: Operational Security Management in Violent Environments: A Field Manual for Aid Agencies*, London: Overseas Development Institute, 2000.
5. Adele Harmer et al. (eds), *Good Practice Review 8: Operational Security Management in Violent Environments*, revised ed., London: Overseas Development Institute, 2010.
6. Harmer et al. (eds), op. cit., p. 1.

7. See Chapter 4, p. 55.

8. Koenraad Van Brabant, "Mainstreaming the Organisational Management of Safety and Security. A Review of Aid Agency Practices and a Guide for Management", London: Overseas Development Institute, March 2001, p. 16.

9. Shaun Bickley, *Safety First: A Safety and Security Handbook for Aid Workers*, 2nd ed., London: Save the Children, 2010, p. vii.

10. Harmer et al. (eds), op. cit., p. 1.

11. Office of the United Nations Security Coordinator, *Security in the Field: Information for Staff Members of the United Nations System*, New York: United Nations, 1998, p. 1.

12. Harmer et al. (eds), op. cit., p. 7.

13. Van Brabant, *Good Practice Review 8: Operational Security Management in Violent Environments: A Field Manual for Aid Agencies*, op. cit., p. 9.

14. Ibid., p. 6.

15. Van Brabant, "Mainstreaming the Organisational Management of Safety and Security: A Review of Aid Agency Practices and a Guide for Management", op. cit., p. 50.

16. Ibid., p. 49.

17. Ibid., p. 17.

18. Harmer et al. (eds), op. cit., p. 1.

19. Harmer et al (eds), op. cit., p. xviii

20. Van Brabant, *Good Practice Review 8: Operational Security Management in Violent Environments: A Field Manual for Aid Agencies*, op. cit., pp. xii–xiii.

21. Harmer et al. (eds), op. cit., p. 7.

22. Ibid., p. 3.

23. Ibid., p. 7.

24. Cutts and Dingle, op. cit., p. 11.

25. Ibid.

26. Lloyd Roberts, op. cit., p. 16.

27. Charles Rogers and Brian Sytsma, *A Shield About Me: Safety Awareness for World Vision Staff*, Monrovia, CA: World Vision, 1998, Cutts and Dingle, op. cit.

28. Van Brabant, *Good Practice Review 8: Operational Security Management in Violent Environments: A Field Manual for Aid Agencies*, op. cit., p. 9.

29. Harmer et al. (eds), op. cit., p. 8.

30. Ibid., p. 35.

31. Van Brabant, *Good Practice Review 8: Operational Security Management in Violent Environments: A Field Manual for Aid Agencies*, op. cit., pp. 22–25.

32. Ibid., pp. 26–35.

33. Ibid., p. xiv; Harmer et al. (eds), op. cit., p. xix.

34. Harmer et al. (eds), op. cit., pp. 39–40.

35. Ibid., p. 101.

36. Ibid., p. 101.

37. Ibid., p. 29.

38. Ibid., p. 27.

39. Ibid., p. xviii.

40. Ibid., p. xv.

41. Ibid., p. 60.

42. Ibid., pp. 60–61.

43. Ibid., pp. 61–63.

44. Ibid., p. 62.

45. Ibid., p. 68.

46. Ibid., pp. 159–160.

47. Van Brabant, *Good Practice Review: Operational Security Management in Violent Environments: A Field Manual for Aid Agencies*, op. cit., p. 56.

48. Harmer et al. (eds), op. cit., p. 71.

49. Ibid., p. 73.

50. Ibid., p. 74.

51. Ibid., p. xix.

52. Ibid., p. 115.

53. Ibid., p. 124.

54. Ibid., p. 131.

55. François Giovalucchi and Jean-Pierre Olivier de Sardan, "Planification, gestion et politique dans l'aude au développement: le cadre logique, outil et miroir des développeurs," *Revue Tiers Monde*, 2, No. 198 (2009).

56. Van Brabant, *Good Practice Review 8: Operational Security Management in Violent Environments: A Field Manual for Aid Agencies*, op. cit., p. xii.

57. Harmer et al. (eds), op. cit., p. xviii.

58. "Introduction", Robert Macpherson and Bennett Pafford, *Care International Safety & Security Handbook*, Geneva: CARE International, 2000.

59. UNSECOORD and UNHCR, *Security Awareness: An Aide-Mémoire*, Geneva: UNHCR, 1995.

60. James Ferguson, *The Anti-Politics Machine: "Development", Depoliticization, and Bureaucratic Power in Lesotho*, Cambridge: Cambridge University Press, 1990.

61. External legal advice to MSF-Australia, 2014.

62. Ian Eddington, *An historical explanation of the development of occupational health and safety and the important position it now occupies in society*, Brisbane: Queensland Safety Forum, January 2006.

63. And internationally, as seen in the International Labour Organisation's Occupational Health and Safety Conventions of 1981 and 2006.

64. French Labour Code, L-4121–1.

65. Cour de cassation, judgment n°2575, 7 December 2011, Société Sanofi Pasteur/ Peyret".

66. A network of international humanitarian aid and development agencies.

67. Duty of care was one of the ten Humanitarian Accountability Project Standard Principles first drafted in 2007. The ICRC began to formally adopt duty of care language in 2009 after a series of critical incidents.

68. For example, Humanitarian HR Conference Europe 2012, "What Duties? Who Cares?", Amsterdam, and InterAction Duty of Care symposium 2014, Washington D.C., which included a presentation by MSF-Holland's HR manager.

69. Edward Kemp and Maarten Merkelbach, "Can you get sued? Legal liability of international humanitarian aid organisations toward their staff", Policy Paper 74, Geneva: Security Management Institute, 2011, p. 17.

70. See the "Karachi litigation case".

71. See Samaritan's Purse vs Flavia Wagner, http://www.reuters.com/article/2011/05/19/us-newyork-kidnap-idUSTRE74I70A20110519, last accessed 30 December 2015. However, as Carolyn Klamp has pointed out, the low number of reported cases could be due to the prevalence of confidential legal settlements. Carolyn Klamp and Associates, "Duty of Care", RedR Safety and Security Review Issue 7, 2007. More recently a court in Oslo has found the Norwegian Refugee Council guilty of gross negligence in its handling of the kidnapping of Steve Dennis and three other staff members in Dadaab, Kenya in 2012, http://www.irinnews.org/report/102243/nrc-kidnap-ruling-is-wake-up-call-for-aid-industry, last accessed 30 December 2015.

72. See Chapter 5, p. 71.

73. For example, boards have voiced their concern regarding their liability in the event of international staff becoming fatally infected with Ebola and, less urgently, in relation to the exposure to asbestos of international staff working in the field. Jonathan Edwards, "Duty of Care in MSF", Internal Report, Medical Care Under Fire, Paris: MSF, 2015.

74. "Guidelines for NGO Professional Safety & Security Risk Management", Dublin: Irish Aid, 2013, p. 1.

6. THE DUTY OF A HEAD OF MISSION: INTERVIEW WITH DELPHINE CHEDORGE, MSF EMERGENCY COORDINATOR IN CENTRAL AFRICAN REPUBLIC

1. This article is based on interviews conducted between May and July 2015. Translated from French by Karen Tucker.

2. "International activity report 2014", Paris: MSF.

3. See, in particular, International Federation for Human Rights, "Central African Republic: They must all leave or die", Press Release, June 2014.

4. We will use the term "ex-Seleka" to describe the Seleka forces who are still active after they were disbanded by a decision of President Michel Djotodia in September 2013 following an increase in violent attacks and abuses.

5. See, in particular, Human Rights Watch report, "'They came to kill us': Escalating atrocities in the Central African Republic", 19 December 2013.
6. Following violent attacks in December 2013, tens of thousands of displaced persons originally from Bangui assembled at the city's airport, Bangui–M'Poko.
7. This refers to Central African staff who are mainly hired in Bangui and then relocated by MSF to programmes in other parts of the country.
8. See Chapter 4, box: "Security Incident Narratives Buried in Numbers: The MSF Example", p. 67.
9. A full account of the research was published in the *Journal of Humanitarian Affairs*, in February 2014: Michaël Neuman, "'No patients, no problems': Exposure to risk of medical personnel working in MSF projects in Yemen's governorate of Amran", https://sites.tufts.edu/jha/archives/2040, last accessed 30 December 2015.
10. Interview with the Amran project coordinator.
11. Located in the north of the country, the governorate has a population of around 1 million inhabitants.
12. Interview with a member of hospital management, Khamer.
13. Interview with a hospital director, Sanaa.
14. Interview with an international doctor, Khamer.
15. Interview with a Yemeni doctor, MSF, Khamer.
16. Interview with a Yemeni doctor, MSF, Khamer.
17. Interview with a Yemeni doctor, former MSF employee, Sanaa.
18. The concepts of "tribe", "sub-tribe" and "family" in the context of Yemen are the subject of academic debate. As Paul Dresch puts it in "Tribalisme et démocratie au Yémen" (*Arabian Humanities*, no. 2, 1994), tribes are "evidently, not [...] very solid group[s]". Although central to the understanding of social and political dynamics, the tribe is a malleable concept: "a very important flexibility in term of conflicts and alliances potentially exists."
19. Interview, June 2013. See also Nadwa Al Dawsari, "Tribal governance and Stability in Yemen", Carnegie Endowment for International Peace, 2012.
20. "Yemeni doctors cause more harm than good", *National Yemen*, 18 July 2012.
21. Ibid.
22. The maternity, paediatric and adult medical departments admit non-emergency patients; patients with leishmaniosis and rickets are also provided with non-emergency treatment.
23. Interview with an international midwife, Amran.

7. QABASSIN, SYRIA: SECURITY ISSUES AND PRACTICES IN AN MSF MISSION IN THE LAND OF JIHAD

1. Translated from French by Philippa Bowe Smith.
2. To avoid any confusion arising from successive changes in staff, we will indicate in

the footnotes the period during which a particular project coordinator or head of mission was present.

3. To explore these questions, we consulted all the literature produced by the Qabassin mission: field reports ("sitreps"), security documents ("security guidelines") and, especially, daily emails exchanged with the coordination team. Interviews with over twenty people involved on the ground, in the coordination team and at the head office in Paris were also conducted between January and June 2015. We thank them for their time and their help. This study does not include any views from the team's Syrian personnel, fascinating as it would have been to have heard their opinions on the situations they faced, the decisions taken and various people's attitudes. For reasons of feasibility, this was always going to be the case.

4. In the end, MSF-Spain opened a project in the "industrial district" on the outskirts of Aleppo in mid-2013.

5. Interview with the head of mission (January–June 2013), 17 June 2015.

6. Bravo [Qabassin] sitrep, week 7–8, 15 to 28 February 2013.

7. Bravo sitrep, week 3–4, January 2013.

8. Security Guidelines—annex 3—Bravo risk analysis, 26 March 2013.

9. Security Guidelines—annex 2—Bravo rules, 26 March 2013.

10. Bravo Security Memo, summary of the rules accompanying the Security Guidelines, 26 March 2013.

11. Security Guidelines, annex 2.

12. See Chapter 5, p. 71.

13. Interviews with the head of mission (January–June 2013), 17 June 2015, and deputy head of mission (June 2013), 6 February 2015.

14. Email exchanges between the logistics coordinator and the project coordinator on 4 June, 6 June, 9 June 2013, etc. This security contact had not been put in place beforehand: "What for? We talked to each other all the time anyway," said the project coordinator who set up the project (December 2012–April 2013).

15. Interview with the project coordinator (April–July 2013), 17 June 2015.

16. We will use the more common acronym: ISIS (the group took its present name, Islamic State (IS), in June 2014).

17. Bravo sitrep week 26–27, 25 July 2013.

18. Email from the head of mission to the project coordinator, 13 August 2013.

19. Email from the project coordinator to the head of mission, 17 August 2013.

20. End of mission report, project coordinator (August–September 2013).

21. Ibid.

22. Late that night, having interviewed all the team members, they applied the same process to themselves and interviewed each other in order to avoid prejudging their respective decisions (discussions with the project coordinator, March 2015).

23. Reported by the project coordinator, interview, 23 June 2015.

24. Exchange of emails between the project coordinator and head of mission, 19 August 2013.

25. Email from the project coordinator to the head of mission, 25 August 2013. As well as using the Internet, the project coordinator asked the medical adviser to show him how to use Twitter so that he could track statements and rumours circulating on that platform.

26. ISIS letter, cited in email from the project coordinator to the head of mission, 20 August 2013.

27. Interview, 23 June 2015.

28. Interview with the project coordinator (April–June 2013), 17 June 2015.

29. "For some groups in the area, being a Buddhist is really as bad as being a Yezidi (...) it can turn nasty." Interview with the project coordinator, 23 June 2015.

30. "I worried about loads of dying people pounding on our door," remembers the physiotherapist based in Atmah, where a similar situation arose (interview, 11 February 2015).

31. Document attached to an email from the project coordinator to the head of mission, 23 August 2013.

32. Email from the project coordinator to the head of mission, 25 August 2013. Two weeks later, heavy fighting broke out in Al-Bab between several political groups including ISIS (which was in the process of establishing a major presence), upsetting the balance of power and thus undermining the appeal of this option.

33. Interview with the president (formerly head of the emergency desk), 20 May 2015.

34. Interview with the outreach doctor, 28 January 2015; informal discussion with the project coordinator, March 2015.

35. Informal discussion, 20 January 2015. "I've never thought of security as a geographical concept," he says. "It's all about finding the right network."

36. Bravo sitrep, August 2013.

37. "MSF in the land of Al-Qaeda", document attached to an email from the project coordinator to the head of mission, 23 August 2013.

38. He had even been the subject of a fatwa issued by an FSA affiliate and MSF-Spain had sent him to Turkey; two months later, wanting to return and claiming the fatwa had been lifted, subject to his good conduct, he returned to Syria, but apparently continued posting his atheist conceptions on Facebook.

39. Incident report, MSF-Spain, 7 September 2013.

40. Email from the project coordinator to the head of mission, 7 September 2013.

41. This was the fourth MSF project to come under ISIS control, along with Qabassin (MSF-France, Aleppo governorate), Tal Abyad (MSF-Holland, Raqqah governorate) and Bernas (MSF-Belgium, Idlib governorate, which fell under ISIS control on 26 August 2013).

42. Email from the project coordinator to the head of mission, 25 September 2013.

43. Incident report, 13 October 2013.

44. That is, the head of mission from mid-September to mid-November 2013 (present since the end of August as deputy).

45. Email from the project coordinator to the head of mission, 21 October 2013, in which he describes the team's stress levels about the situation as excessive, and emails from the head of mission to the project coordinator, 22 October.

46. Interview with the head of mission (mid-September–mid-November), 25 February 2015.

47. Interview, 27 January 2015.

48. Interview with the medical advisor present in October and November 2013, 4 June 2015.

49. Interview with the president, 20 May 2015.

50. Exchange of emails between the head of mission and the project coordinator, 22 October 2013.

51. Project coordinator present from December 2013 to February 2014 (the mission's fifth). Having already worked in Qabassin in August as a logistics officer, then with the coordination team in October–November, he was one of the "pessimists".

52. Email from the logistics coordinator to the project coordinator, 23 December 2013.

53. Interview with the head of the emergency desk since June 2013, 28 January 2015.

54. Ibid.

8. THE SHADOWY THEATRE OF KIDNAPPINGS: AN ACCOUNT OF ARJAN ERKEL'S RESCUE

1. Dutch journalist Coen van Zwol has written a history of the kidnapping and Erkel himself has published a memoir of his time in captivity, both of which are referred to in this text. See Coen van Zwol, *Gijzelaar van de Kaukasus: De ontvoering van Arjan Erkel*, Amsterdam/Rotterdam: Prometheus, 2005; and Arjan Erkel, *Ontvoerd: 607 dagen tussen leven en dood* (*My Abduction: 607 Days Between Life and Death*), Amsterdam: Uitgeverij Balans, 2005.

2. Various estimates put the number of Chechens dead or missing between 50,000 and 100,000 out of an initial population estimated at around 1 million people. See Thorniké Gordadze, "Chechnya: Eradication of the Enemy Within", in Fabrice Weissman (ed.), *In the Shadow of "Just Wars": Violence, Politics and Humanitarian Action*, London: Hurst & Co., 2004, pp. 183–208.

3. Amnesty International report, "Russian Federation: What justice for Chechnya's disappeared?", May 2007.

4. Reports such as "The Chechen Republic, Far from Peace", released in 1996, detailed the "systematic bombing and killing of civilians by the Russian military in Chechnya" while the November 2000 report "Chechnya: Politics of Terror" denounced the "massive aggressions and the policy of terror towards the civilians of Chechnya".

5. This total includes twelve "express kidnapping" (resolved in less than 24 hours) and four extended-period abductions of which Erkel's was the longest.

6. FIDH and Centre des droits de l'Homme de Memorial, "Rapport d'enquête sur les crimes de guerre et les crimes contre l'humanité perpétrés en Tchétchénie", October 2000.

7. Véronique Soulé, "Tchétchénie: Vincent Cochetel le miraculé. Enlevé en janvier, le Français a été libéré par les Russes samedi", *Libération*, 14 December 1998.

8. AFP, "Red Cross removes workers from North Caucasus after NZ kidnapping", 24 May 1999.

9. See Laurence Binet, "War crimes and politics of terror in Chechnya, 1994–2004", "MSF Speaking Out" Case Studies, September 2014, p. 161.

10. Coen van Zwol, "Identity of the US Attachés was Unknown to Erkel", *NRC*, 16 July 2003.

11. "In Chechnya, the intensity of violence has not diminished. On the contrary, bombardments, cleansings, rackets, death squads and tortures are the norm", taken from "MSF Concerned Over New Pressures Exerted on Chechen Refugees in Ingushetia to Return to Chechnya", MSF Press Release, 3 June 2002.

12. Van Zwol, op. cit., p. 18. See also Arkady Babchenko's collection *One Soldier's War in Chechnya*, London: Portobello Books, 2007, which also provides detailed anecdotes of the regional economic impact of the conflict.

13. According to the Jamestown Foundation or the BBC for instance, "The kidnapping threat [was] worst in the north Caucasus—in Chechnya and its neighbours, Ingushetia and Dagestan". See Nabi Abdullaev, "Foreigners beware: Kidnappers are still operating in the North Caucasus", The Jamestown Foundation, 27 February 2001; Stephen Mulvey, "Analysis: Caucasus kidnap threat", BBC News Online, 21 June 2002.

14. The reduction and evacuation of international staff occurred progressively within the different sections: the French section suspended all expatriate staff travel in the Caucasus following the initial FSB warning; the Belgian section suspended travel after the kidnapping of Davydovich, as did the Dutch section, although they did maintain a presence in Nalchik, Kabardino–Balkar Republic.

15. Internal MSF document.

16. Ibid.

17. From a French translation of Erkel, op. cit.

18. Internal MSF document.

19. Interview with Thomas Nierle, former director of operations of MSF-Switzerland, 5 May 2015. Setting up an additional crisis cell in the abducted person's country of origin is standard practice within MSF.

20. Christian Democratic Appeal.

21. Internal MSF document.

22. "Positioning on the Arjan Erkel affair in the public domain", MSF internal notes, 2004.

23. See "Russia main oil supplier to the Netherlands", *Statistics Netherlands Web magazine*, 15 March 2004.

24. The more conspiratorial made the link to oil politics in the Caucasus: it was in the interests of Western corporations to fuel chaos in Dagestan and foster stability in Georgia in order to promote Georgia as the main transport hub for Caspian oil and gas. Van Zwol, Gijzelaar van de Kaukasus, op. cit., pp. 11–12, 66.

25. "Résurgence des activités des rebelles tchétchènes", *Le Figaro*, 21 August 2002.

26. The need to exercise patience and discretion in order to facilitate the resolution of an abduction through a secret commercial transaction is one of the main recommendations delivered during trainings on kidnap management, cf. MSF-France Internal Training, "Abduction and kidnapping", run by a former head of Scotland Yard's Hostage And Crisis Negotiation Unit, Paris, 12–13 June 2013. This recommendation corresponds to the good practices endorsed by kidnapping specialists. See interview with Alain Juillet, former intelligence director at the DGSE and senior advisor for Orrick Rambaud Martel, in Ministry of the Interior, "Business en milieu hostile. La protection des entreprises à l'international", *Défis*, no. 2, 2014, p. 11; Dorothée Moisan, *Rançons. Enquête sur le business des otages*, Paris: Fayard, 2013, pp. 91–95; Brynna Leslie, "In Harm's Way", *Canadian Insurance Risk Manager*, summer 2011.

27. For instance the letter from Thomas Linde, general director of MSF-Switzerland, and Morten Rostrup, president of the International Council of MSF, to the ambassador of Russia in Switzerland, 23 August 2002.

28. "MSF Condemns Kidnapping of Relief Worker—Operations in Chechnya, Dagestan and Ingushetia Suspended", MSF Press Release, 14 August 2002.

29. Medical staff practiced mouth-to-mouth resuscitation due to the large numbers of patients with respiratory distress and the lack of resuscitation bags.

30. Interview (2009) with Anne Fouchard, former deputy communications director of MSF-France, in Binet, op. cit., p. 231.

31. MSF internal document.

32. Interview (2009) with Thomas Nierle, in Binet, op. cit., p. 216.

33. Interview (2009) with Jean-Hervé Bradol, former president of MSF-France, in Binet, op. cit., p. 229. The message that "Arjan got what he deserved" was repeated in May 2003 by an assistant director of the FSB during a meeting with the Dutch ambassador and MSF-Switzerland director of operations. Interview (2009) with Thomas Nierle, in ibid., p. 255.

34. CRG had already provided advice to the Dutch section on basic training and crisis protocols prior to Arjan's abduction, as well as during Kenny Gluck's abduction.

35. "CIA without Borders" and "Doctors without Medicines" were already common epithets for MSF within the Russian army and secret services. See van Zwol, "Identity of the US Attachés was Unknown to Erkel", op. cit.

36. Interview (2009) with Thomas Nierle, in Binet, op. cit., p. 232.

37. "Implementing Phase 2—Rough draft", MSF-Switzerland crisis cell, 13 January 2003.

38. MSF internal document.

39. Letter from Jaap de Hoop Scheffer, minister of foreign affairs of the Kingdom of the Netherlands, to Morten Rostrup, president of the International Council of MSF, 29 January 2003; minutes of Arjan Erkel meeting, Ministry of Foreign Affairs, The Hague, 29 January 2003.

40. Interview (2009) with Rafa Vila San Juan, former MSF International Secretary General, in Binet, op. cit., p. 245.

41. "Arjan Erkel, Abducted Six Months Ago in Dagestan, Is Still Missing: MSF Calls on the Russian and Dagestani Governments to Give High Political Priority to the Case", MSF Press Release, 12 February 2003.

42. "Birthday of Arjan, an MSF Volunteer who has been Held Hostage for Seven Months in the Caucasus, Marked by an International Appeal for his Release: Russian Authorities not Facing up to their Responsibilities", MSF Press Release, 7 March 2003.

43. Fenneken Veldkamp and Coen van Zwol, "A Young Fair-haired Man is Worth Millions in Dagestan", NRC, 5 April 2003.

44. van Zwol, Gijzelaar van de Kaukasus, op. cit., p. 14.

45. van Zwol, "Identity of the US Attachés was Unknown to Erkel", op. cit. According to Erkel's memoir, the kidnappers also claimed to have noticed the FSB tail.

46. Internal MSF document.

47. An exception during this relatively quiet period was the EU summit meeting during which Erkel's fate was raised publicly by President Putin and Dutch Prime Minister Jan Peter Balkenende. "EU Pledges Support for Russia's Peace Plan in Chechnya", AFP, 31 May 2003.

48. Internal MSF document.

49. Ibid.

50. "One year after Arjan Erkel's Kidnapping, MSF Considers the Investigation to be a Failure and Calls for more Action by the Russian Authorities to Resolve the Case", MSF Press Release, 12 August 2003.

51. Internal MSF document.

52. Bob Herbert, "Kindness's Cruel Reward", editorial, The New York Times, 26 September 2003.

53. See Coen van Zwol, "Identity of Arjan Erkel's Kidnapper is Known", NRC, 5 November 2003, and Coen van Zwol, "Death for the Living", NRC, 16 November 2003.

54. Internal MSF document.

55. Jean-Hervé Bradol and Pierre Salignon, "Arjan Erkel: enlèvement politique et mensonge d'Etat", Revue Humanitaire, no. 11, 2004.

56. "Crisis Cell Communication Plan", February–May 2004. Of note, earlier lobbying had focused on the Russian Minister of Foreign Affairs Ivanov, Italy via Berlusconi, the Mexican government as chair of the UN Security Council, Kofi

Annan, Condoleeza Rice and Colin Powell. The latter period had targeted Sergei Lavrov in particular, as he was assumed to be close to President Putin.

57. Interview (2009) with Kenny Gluck, former director of operations of MSF-Holland, in Binet, op. cit., p. 286.
58. "Embargo on Communications Campaign", MSF correspondence, 26 February 2004.
59. "Arjan Erkel, Hostage in the Russian Federation since August 12, 2002", MSF Press Pack, 1 March 2004.
60. From a "source" in early February 2004, internal MSF document. It was later concluded by the team in charge of evaluating the management of Arjan's kidnap, that this news was "a form of deliberate disinformation" by the kidnappers (of course, this was not known at the time) that provoked panic within MSF-Switzerland and the advisory group.
61. See "MSF: Officials Implicated in the Kidnapping of the MSF Representative in Dagestan", AFP, 9 March 2004; "MSF Accuses Russian Officials of Keeping one of Their Volunteers Hostage", Le Monde, 10 March 2004; "Médecins Sans Frontières Accuses Russian Authorities of Complicity in Abduction of Aid Worker", Associated Press, 11 March 2004.
62. "Russia Officially Accused over Kidnappings—MSF Makes Unpleasant Statements", Nezavisimaya Gazeta, 11 March 2004.
63. "Arjan Erkel, Coordinator of the Médecins Sans Frontières has been Released in Dagestan," RIA Novosti, 11 April 2004.
64. Van Zwol, Gijzelaar van de Kaukasus, op. cit., p. 114.
65. See the minutes of the MSF-France Board of Directors meeting, 26 March 2004. As MSF rejected its claim for reimbursement, the Dutch State decided to sue the organisation's Swiss section. After four years of legal proceedings and two rulings in favour of MSF in the court of first instance and then in the court of appeal, Switzerland's Federal Tribunal ruled partially in favour of the Dutch State by pronouncing that the financial burden of the ransom should be shared between the two parties. "It is unacceptable to ask a humanitarian organisation to share the cost of a ransom negotiated and paid by a government. By agreeing to downgrade the consequences of the abduction of a humanitarian worker to a mere commercial dispute, as requested by the Dutch government, the Federal Tribunal's ruling is contributing to making unpunished crimes against humanitarian workers—which have become more frequent in recent years—part of everyday life", commented MSF. MSF Press Release, "Appalling Ruling in Court Case Between Dutch Government and MSF", 14 July 2008.
66. From a French translation of Erkel, op. cit.
67. Simon Ostrovsky, "Light is Shed on Erkel's Release", The Moscow Times, 15 April 2004.
68. Interview with Jean-Hervé Bradol, former president of MSF-France, 26 June 2015.

69. Letter, Linde and Rostrup, to the ambassador of Russia in Switzerland, op. cit.

70. Interview with Michiel Hofman, former MSF-Holland head of mission in Russia, 25 June 2015.

71. Interview with Steve Cornish, former head of the Moscow-based crisis cell, MSF-Switzerland, 29 May 2015.

72. "Arjan Erkel is Still Being Held Hostage After One Year", MSF Press Release, op. cit.

73. Among the three other MSF employees who were detained for a long period in the Caucasus, one escaped, one was released without conditions, and the third was exchanged for a relatively small sum of money.

INDEX

175

INDEX

INDEX

FONDATION **MÉDECINS SANS FRONTIÈRES**

crash | CENTRE DE RÉFLEXION SUR L'ACTION ET LES SAVOIRS HUMANITAIRES

The Centre de Réflexion sur l'Action et les Savoirs Humanitaires (MSF-CRASH) was created in 1995 by the French section of MSF and is hosted by the MSF Foundation. Its objective is to encourage critical reflection on the humanitarian practices of the association in order to improve its action.

The CRASH team consists of four to five permanent employees, all with field and headquarters experience and a university background. MSF-CRASH members are supported by a scientific committee made up of volunteer professional academics. They work in close cooperation with the president, the management team and the operational directors of Médecins Sans Frontières.

CRASH team members undertake and supervise studies and analyses on MSF actions and their environment. They participate in assessment missions in the field and in internal training sessions. They represent the association at meetings, conferences and research forums, and participate in the public debate on the stakes, constraints, limits and dilemmas of humanitarian action.

For more information on CRASH: www.msf-crash.org

Founded in 1971, Médecins Sans Frontières is an international medical humanitarian organisation that delivers emergency aid to people affected by armed conflict, epidemics, natural disasters and exclusion from healthcare.

MSF is a movement comprised of 21 sections based in Australia, Austria, Belgium, Brazil, Canada, Denmark, France, Germany, Greece, Holland, Hong Kong, Italy, Japan, Luxembourg, Norway, the United Kingdom, South Africa, Spain, Sweden, Switzerland and the United States. Each section has its own associative structure answering to a Board of Directors elected by members during an Annual General Assembly. MSF has five operational centres in France, Belgium, Holland, Spain and Switzerland and offices in Argentina, the Czech Republic, India, Ireland, Mexico, South Korea and the United Arabic Emirates. Its International Secretariat is based in Geneva. Each section defines, in keeping with MSF's charter and a series of agreements ratified by all the sections, its own intervention strategies.

MSF's financial autonomy affords the organisation great flexibility. Almost 90 per cent of its resources come from private, non-governmental funding. In 2014, over 5.7 million donors contributed to MSF funding, for a total of €1.3 billion. In addition, €115 million were collected from public institutional agencies. MSF spending for the year amounted to $1.07 billion.

The largest projects, in terms of cost, were in South Sudan, the Democratic Republic of Congo, Central African Republic and in West Africa, where MSF responded to the Ebola epidemic. Over half of MSF's programmes were conducted in situations of armed conflict and the rest in stable settings. These projects were carried out by over 36,000 staff—doctors, nurses, logisticians, administrators, epidemiologists, laboratory technicians, etc.—most of whom are based in their home countries. They work in close collaboration with colleagues in the various sections and offices, such as programme managers and medical, logistics and administrative support teams, who define with the field teams the organisation's objectives as well as the resources required to implement them.

For more information on Médecins Sans Frontières: www.msf.org

THE CHARTER OF MÉDECINS SANS FRONTIÈRES

Médecins Sans Frontières is a private international organisation. Most of its members are doctors and health workers, but many other support professions contribute to MSF's smooth functioning. All of them agree to honour the following principles:

Médecins Sans Frontières offers assistance to populations in distress, to victims of natural or man-made disasters and to victims of armed conflict without discrimination and irrespective of race, religion, creed or political affiliation.

Médecins Sans Frontières observes neutrality and impartiality in the name of universal medical ethics and the right to humanitarian assistance and demands full and unhindered freedom in the exercise of its functions.

Médecins Sans Frontières' volunteers undertake to respect their professional code of ethics and to maintain complete independence from all political, economic and religious powers.

As volunteers, members are aware of the risks and dangers of the missions they undertake, and have no right to compensation for themselves or their beneficiaries other than that which Médecins Sans Frontières is able to afford them.